TENSION
BETWEEN
OPPOSITES

TENSION BETWEEN OPPOSITES

*Reflections on the Practice
and Theory of Politics*

PAUL H. NITZE

CHARLES SCRIBNER'S SONS • NEW YORK
MAXWELL MACMILLAN CANADA • TORONTO
MAXWELL MACMILLAN INTERNATIONAL
NEW YORK • OXFORD • SINGAPORE • SYDNEY

Charles Scribner's Sons
Macmillan Publishing Company
866 Third Avenue
New York, NY 10022

Maxwell Macmillan Canada, Inc.
1200 Eglinton Avenue East
Suite 200
Don Mills, Ontario M3C 3N1

Macmillan Publishing Company is part of the Maxwell Communication Group of Companies.

Library of Congress Cataloging-in-Publication Data
Nitze, Paul H.
Tension between opposites : reflections on the practice and theory of politics / Paul H. Nitze
p.   cm.
Includes bibliographical references (p.   ) and index.
ISBN 0-684-19628-X
1. United States—Foreign relations—1993
I. Title.
E885.N57   1993   93-12874
327.73—dc20   CIP

Macmillan books are available at special discounts for bulk purchases for sales promotions, premiums, fund-raising, or educational use. For details, contact:
Special Sales Director
Macmillan Publishing Company
866 Third Avenue
New York, NY 10022

10   9   8   7   6   5   4   3   2   1

Printed in the United States of America

CONTENTS

CONTENTS

ACKNOWLEDGMENTS

This book had its origin in a seminar at the School of Advanced International Studies of The Johns Hopkins University, which I chaired for a number of years. The subject of the seminar was "Toward Illuminating the Theory and Practice of Politics," in the classical Greek sense of the word "politics." Specifically, we attempted to refine year by year an outline of the subject matter as it had evolved from the efforts of earlier groups of participating graduate students. In those days, Kenneth Thompson, of the Rockefeller Foundation and later director of the Miller Center at the University of Virginia, helped us obtain financial support for the project. He had attempted to use our outline in teaching his own students but found it much too elliptical to be of real value. Kenneth caused me to attempt to translate our evolving outline into a book. For all of this I wish to acknowledge a particular debt to him. I also wish to thank Ann Smith, then my secretary, who provided direction and a record of our work; she later contributed to the research.

Harold Evans, at the time editor of the *Atlantic Monthly* magazine and publisher of the Atlantic Monthly Press, took a strong interest in our project. The *Atlantic Monthly* was acquired by Mortimer Zuckerman, and Harry became for a short time publisher of *U.S. News & World Report* and then of Newhouse Publication's *Traveler* magazine. During this tumultuous period for him, he continued to spend half a day each week in reviewing the work that Ann Smith and I were doing to convert the outline on the theory and practice of politics into a book. It was his intention, after he had mastered the subject, to write the book himself. He rightly doubted my facility as an author. But, eventually, he found he couldn't spare the time and energy to get it done. So, we divided the task into two parts. One was to be a book describing my extended negotiations with the Russians and focusing on defense and arms control issues, which eventually appeared as *From Hiroshima to Glasnost*. The other was to be this book on the theory and practice of politics.

With respect to this book, I especially wish to thank James McCall, my able research assistant from SAIS, who helped me with the writing necessary to assure that it bears relation to historical fact and to the realities of logic. From the beginning James had an outstanding grasp of my theoretical approach and a solid understanding of what I was trying to accomplish. I tend to write from recollection and insight as the spirit moves me; he has attempted to keep me in continuous touch with reality. James McCall fully deserves to be considered a coauthor.

Patricia Hass encouraged me in establishing the connection with Scribner's. She believed in my book even though at that time it was in very preliminary form.

At some point or another, some of my friends read parts of the manuscript and made invaluable comments. They are: Ted Lewis, president of St. Mary's College; C. B. Marshall, a philosopher and man of action; Mary Carswell, director of the Mac-Dowell Colony; former Secretary of State George Shultz; Dr. Milton Heifetz of Boston College Law School, and my daughter Nina Thompson, an art historian.

Jim Thomas, who joined us as my student assistant in the last few months of the project, efficiently contributed to the research and editing.

I am also grateful to the SAIS Library for providing reference material whenever necessary. The National Archives and the Library of Congress also provided guidance and information to my researchers.

I am particularly grateful to my special assistant, Maria Valle, who added this project to her tasks with great enthusiasm. She took responsibility for keyboarding the manuscript, making suggestions concerning its substance and style, and she effectively coordinated all the components that went into making the project possible.

Finally, I owe much to Robert Stewart, the publisher and editor of Scribner's. He gave me continuous confidence and support but also questioned all complicating excursions and explanations that would have diverted the reader from the main themes. He helped me reduce what would have been a book of some six hundred pages to less than half that length with no loss of substance and with an increase in precision and, I believe, clarity.

To all of the individuals mentioned above I am deeply grateful for their interest and support. It is needless to say that the responsibility for all errors is mine.

PREFACE

A number of things can be said of this, the twentieth century. Ours has been a century of vast human, physical, and—particularly—political and cultural destruction. It has also been a century of enormous growth, not only in population and in scientific and technical knowledge, but also of world community. It has seen the mutual destruction of the European empires that dominated the world at the outset of the century, the rise of totalitarian drives for dominance, and finally the triumph of liberal political and economic practices. The United States has played an increasingly influential role in these developments.

In this book, I attempt to develop a set of ideas that, in sum, prick out a way of looking at political problems: ideas appropriate to the last decade of the century. The emphasis is on political problems among sovereign states, but the politics across national boundaries are driven as much by domestic issues and the ambitions, character, and prejudices of individuals as they are by the interests of nations. So, it is to the theory and practice of politics in its broadest sense that this work is directed.

The ideas I advance here derive in large measure from long-continuing and intense discussions with a number of individuals with whom the accidents of history threw me into close contact. Some of my ideas toward a theory of politics have appeared elsewhere, and where this is the case I have so noted in the text. Some of the events that brought about those contacts are described in *From Hiroshima to Glasnost*.[1]

I have not hesitated to draw from those memoirs where I thought to do so would add to the clarity of these essays.

In advancing a series of ideas that I hope will illuminate important aspects of political theory and practice, I make no claim to novelty. I am sure that others can find antecedents for most, if not all, of these ideas. But most, if not all, have also been matters of serious controversy. I choose to believe that these essays apply common sense to a complex and difficult subject.

[1] Nitze, Paul H. with Ann M. Smith and Stephen L. Rearden. *From Hiroshima to Glasnost: At the Center of Decision—A Memoir* (New York: Grove Weidenfeld, 1989).

INTRODUCTION

ON THE TWENTIETH— THE AMERICAN— CENTURY

From the Congress of Vienna in 1815 to the beginning of the twentieth century, Great Britain, with its island position, superior navy, and worldwide colonies, had so thrown its weight in the political scales as to keep any hegemonic challenger—France, Germany, or Russia—from becoming dominant in Europe. Beyond Europe as well, for nearly a century Britain influenced and managed events, creating order and stability for commerce, sometimes altruistically, sometimes not. By the outset of the twentieth century, fresh from the success and acquisitions of the Spanish-American War, Americans began to become aware of the potential similar power of the United States to affect world events. They also became aware of a certain responsibility to use that power wisely. However, as a nation, Americans wished to keep their distance from the struggles of Europeans, hesitating to become embroiled in their power squabbles, concentrating instead on interests closer to home.

As the century passed through two world wars and some forty years of cold war, the United States emerged in the 1990s into a world radically changed from that of 1900. One by one, the empires that had constituted the balance of power in Europe during the nineteenth century were overwhelmed by war or other political events. Imperial Russia, Austria-Hungary, and the Ottoman Empire did not survive the First World War; Germany in defeat lost her colonies and part of her traditional homeland; Britain, France, and Italy, although victors, survived but gravely wounded. Between the wars, as the old European powers began to recover unsteadily, the United States and the new Soviet Union, organized on quite opposed political principles, emerged as the two rising powers.

With the end of the Second World War, and the destruction of the hegemonic attempts of Nazi Germany, Fascist Italy, and a militaristic Japan, these once rising powers found themselves at the heads of rival ideological and military alliances. On the one side was the Soviet Union, its allies and satellites dedicated to the eventual triumph of Marxist-Leninist doctrines; on the other was the United States, supporting a wide coalition of non-Marxist-Leninist states. The two sides struggled over the survival of their competing ideological systems. It was a political conflict based in part upon—and in part fueled by—important scientific, intellectual, demographic, economic, and technological developments.

The twentieth century saw radical changes in the United States as well. At the beginning of the 1900s, the vast cornucopia of burgeoning productivity and the resultant hopeful opportunities for a better life for almost everyone dominated the political view of Americans. By 1990 that productivity had slowed, the opportunities began to disappear, and the frontiers to close in. Americans found themselves in a world with a population too great for the planet to support, a world facing the progressive exhaustion of the natural resources on which the continued well-being of that population depended. They also were confronted by an immense growth in the power and lethality of weapon systems, and with increasingly serious damage to the world environment for plants, animal life, and for man itself. As the end of the American Century approaches, American optimism is tempered with an onslaught of difficult economic and political challenges.

It now appears in the last decade of the twentieth century that the United States, despite its limited area and relatively small population (250 million people) in relation to China, India, the European community, will bear a disproportionate share of the responsibility for what the world will become in the next century.

What useful concepts, what wisdom, can those who have participated in and observed the crucial events of this century distill from their experience and pass on to those who must deal with the issues of the next century? Is it possible to develop a framework of ideas that can illuminate the political problems of the past and give some approximate guidelines for how to deal with analogous problems more effectively in the future? In other words, is it possible to deduce from the practical experiences and wisdom of past generations some theory of politics useful to future practitioners?

It is my view that most of what has been written and taught under the heading of "political science" by Americans since World War II has been contrary to experience and to common sense. It has also been of limited value, if not counterproductive, as a guide to the actual conduct of policy. The study of politics and policy can never be a science; science presupposes certainty, at least within definable limits, demonstrable by repeatable experiments. Politics and policies can never be precisely repeated and analogies are only suggestive. The best that we can strive for is judgment that is more apt to be right than wrong: it can rarely, if ever, produce certainties.

The judgments in this book are necessarily based on ideas and an external world seen through the eyes of one man, myself. As a boy I was excessively shy, awkward, lacking in self-confidence. I lived in a world of ideas, which tended to separate me from my classmates. In business, I found it difficult to put the interests of my firm ahead of all other interests as a true team player was expected to do. In government, I found it hard to be wholly loyal to the principles of either the Democratic party or of the Republican party. I, therefore, never achieved appointment to the highest political offices. I was, in effect, fired from the government four times; three other times I resigned because I found my position to be personally intolerable. Nevertheless, I believe few others have been as fortunate to participate as actively as I have, either as a member of the government team or as an outside critic, in the major decisions on U.S. policy during the critical fifty years from 1940 to 1990.

There is an enormous difference in the intensity with which life is experienced depending upon the historical era in which one is born, the group to which one is or becomes attached, one's position in that group, and the opportunities that group has to seize and to actualize what it senses to be the great inner possibilities of the moment. Few men have had the good fortune to grow up in Athens in the days of Pericles, in Florence in the days of the Medici, or in England in the time of Queen Elizabeth I. Most have lived in less auspicious times when it was necessary to turn the other cheek to those commanding the greater power despite one's doubts as to their worthiness to lead.

Most people in America have avoided oppression or humiliation; some have not. Some have been at the center of America's exploitation of the resources of this continent, the development of the marvels technology has made possible, or the creative opportunities of the arts; others have not. It was only after I came down to Washington in 1940 to work with General George C. Marshall on the draft of the Selective Service Act of that year that I was exposed to the ideals and realities of the American political system. General Marshall was deeply attached to that system and was able to move it in directions he thought necessary for the country as a whole. The education he gave us was invaluable.

It was during my years as director of the State Department's Policy Planning Staff in the Truman and Eisenhower administration from January 1950 to June 1953 that I first felt the impact of full participation in the decisions of the United States as the responsible leader of a coalition of half the world. During that period, we in the Policy Planning Staff were responsible for the central policy staff work and recommendations concerning the Korean War, the Korean armistice negotiations, and the decision to proceed with the development of thermonuclear weapons. As director of the Policy Planning Staff, I headed the drafting and annual revisions of the basic national security document NSC-68, approved by President Truman in 1950. In sum, these documents embodied the core of our political and defense policy for the succeeding forty years. We felt that the full weight of responsibility for the actions to be taken rested upon us in the Staff, and upon me in particular as director of the group. It was we who had done the staff work and we who had put forward the crucial recommendations. To be in the eye of that storm was to be fully alive in a sense vouchsafed to few. We were prime movers in affairs of immense scope.

Early in 1953 I had become a Democrat, and President

Dwight Eisenhower and Secretary of State John Foster Dulles decided in April of that year they needed a new and Republican face as head of the Policy Planning Staff. They first moved me to the Pentagon, but after my confirmation in a new position there became controversial, it was evident that I had no alternative but to offer my resignation. It was accepted in June 1953.

From then until the election of 1960 I had more time and opportunity to think in greater depth about the issues we had faced during the Truman years and on which we had recommended decisions as best we could within the time available. Had those of us been right who had taken such an uncompromising view of the superiority of the liberal Western value system to the opposed claims of those following the Marxist-Leninist-Stalinist doctrine? Had we been right to urge that the U.S. proceed to determine the feasibility of a controlled thermonuclear reaction? Had we been right to judge that the United States was economically strong enough to sustain the role we had recommended? Would the American public sustain that effort long enough to permit the nation to attain its intended aim? By what process of thought, on what evidences of fact, on what lessons of history, judged by what criteria of justice, ethics, or morals could one arrive at answers to such questions?

From a consideration of these difficult questions, there emerged the idea of developing a framework of thought that would constitute the basis for a better, more realistic theory of politics. This framework would help illuminate the subject and might offer some insight into the ethical and moral basis of the practice of politics. What follows are my thoughts, observations, and conclusions about the theory and practice of politics set amid examples I draw from my own personal experience.

1

ON POLITICAL THEORY AND THE TENSION OF OPPOSITES

During the bilateral arms control negotiations with the Soviets from the fall of 1969 until June of 1974, my opposite number on the Soviet side was a distinguished Russian scientist named Alexander Shchukin. Older than I by seven years, he had been born in St. Petersburg in 1900. His father was a well-known geologist and watercolorist who had spent much of his life exploring the mountain ranges south and east of the Urals looking for minerals, sketching as he went. Shchukin's mother was active in politics and during the failed Russian revolution of 1905 became a leading left-wing Communist intellectual.

Alexander early showed musical talent. At first, his family intended that he become a composer, but later decided that he was better endowed to become a conductor of classical music. He had a French governess and spoke excellent French—so good that I had no trouble understanding him. He could even understand my imperfect French.

At seventeen, Shchukin was drafted into the Russian Army as were all his contemporaries of that age. Shortly thereafter, the October Revolution took place and it became necessary for him

to choose between following one of the White generals or becoming part of the Red Army. The Whites were in favor of continuing the war against Germany in accordance with Russia's
commitments to the allies. The Reds were unconditionally for
peace. Shchukin decided Russia needed peace above all else and
sided with the Reds. He fought for five years in the long and bit-
ter civil war. He eventually became the principal radio operator
at Tashkent, from which no communications with Moscow were
possible except by radio. He thus early listened in on significant
discussions among Communist leaders at a high political level.

After the victory of the Reds, Shchukin went to Leningrad
where an uncle who was the head of the local polytechnic institute undertook Shchukin's education in physics. Virtually no scientists had survived both the war against the Germans and the
civil war. One of the few was a Jewish physicist, Abram F. Joffee,
who was the director of a research laboratory in Leningrad. He
asked Shchukin to join him and shortly thereafter put him in
charge of that part of his laboratory studying wave mechanics.
That subject includes the full spectrum of electromagnetic waves
from X rays and radar waves to ultraviolet and infrared light
waves. It also includes sound waves in air and sonar waves in
water. Shchukin quickly mastered the subject and wrote the first
Soviet textbooks on wave mechanics. He also was elected a
member of the Soviet Academy of Sciences at a relatively young
age. Membership in the Academy assured him the perquisites of
an academician regardless of where he chose to work. He had
relatively adequate pay, superior living quarters, and permission
to buy things in the stores reserved for the Nomenklatura.

Shchukin became particularly interested in sonar and moved
to a naval laboratory in Tashkent where he devoted himself to

sonar and to underwater communication. This work brought him into close contact with the Soviet Navy and its submarine fleet. Later, he directed his own research institute in Moscow, the Institute for the Study of Wave Mechanics.

My own contact with Shchukin began in 1969, when the bilateral Strategic Arms Limitation Treaty (SALT) negotiations began between an American team and a Soviet team. Often, during the breaks between formal exchanges at our scheduled meetings, Shchukin and I would go off for a talk between the two of us. We usually didn't use interpreters because we would talk in French. Furthermore, we could speak quite frankly because few, if any, of the KGB people assigned to Shchukin understood what we were saying; they had been chosen for their English skills, not for their French. When we had finished talking about the issues raised in the plenary meeting, we would range over the arts, science, philosophy, and history.

Shchukin was a fascinating man. His knowledge of music was encyclopedic; he knew by heart the scores of most of the important works of classical music, for he had conducted them as a young student conductor. It turned out that our tastes in music were virtually identical. He had a greater interest in Aleksandr Scriabin—a friend of his father's—than I; I had devoted more time to the study of Bach than he. We agreed on when in their careers modern composers, such as Stravinsky, Rachmaninoff, and Mahler, had become overly complex and shocking.

On the philosophy of science our views also converged, though he was far more deeply involved and knowledgeable. However, from my childhood on I had been exposed to scientists; first, to the great physicists and mathematicians associated with the University of Chicago, including Albert A. Michelson,

Robert A. Milliken, and Leonard Dixon, later to the physicists associated with the development of nuclear and other military weapons.

Shchukin was much interested in information theory, particularly in the work of Professor Charles S. Peirce, who had done truly pioneering work in that field at The Johns Hopkins University. An important factor in Peirce's theory was the role of "feedback," the ability of a system (organic or electronic) to correct inaccuracies in the early transmission using information available as the transmission proceeds. We both agreed that certain scientists in the United States, of whom Norbert Weiner was the best known, had attempted to make information theory, particularly its feedback element, the queen of the sciences. Shchukin had had a continuing battle with a group of Soviet scientists who wished to have information theory and feedback dominate Soviet physics. We both considered that their attempt to subordinate physics as a whole to a single part of physics was misguided. It also appeared to us that that attempt had led its proponents into a series of internal contradictions.

While he would speak out on matters of science and the arts, Shchukin was generally cautious in talking about anything touching on the ideological differences between our two countries. At times, however, it became evident that his belief in the probable truth of scientific theory backed by repeatable experiments exceeded his loyalty to Marxist doctrine.

One day, during a period when the talks were taking place in Helsinki, Gerard Smith, head of the U.S. delegation, invited the Soviet delegation to a luncheon at a restaurant on the roof of a building overlooking the main esplanade and looking out to the harbor and the Baltic beyond. After lunch, over coffee, Vladimir Semenov, head of the Soviet delegation, and Smith were trading rather boring stories about philosophers of ancient Greece. I became aware that Shchukin was whispering something in my ear in French.

"I hate philosophers," he said. I whispered back that I did not, that I thought I had learned a great deal from Greek philosophers, particularly Heraclitus and Plato.

"I am not talking about Greek philosophers," he whispered. "They did their best with what they had. I am talking about philosophers popular in my own country."

"To whom are you referring?" I asked.

"To Marx and Engels, of course," he replied. "They relied entirely upon Kant and Hegel who knew nothing about the scientific method; the result has been to set back the development of my country by several generations."

In subsequent discussions we also came to a common understanding that science, mathematics, and the scientific method have their own limitations. The neo-positivists and linguistic analysts, who at that time had become dominant among academic philosophers at Cambridge and Oxford and at a number of campuses in Germany and the United States, had advanced the proposition that truth consisted *only* of those hypotheses whose validity can be demonstrated by repeatable, scientifically rigorous experiments. At a stroke they thereby purported to eliminate the world of policy, of values, of ethics, of "should" propositions from the world of truth and even from its approximation. All such propositions were relegated to "preferences" that could be tabulated and counted but had no inherent merit relative to other preferences. Shchukin and I enjoyed verbally tearing up both the bigots and the relativists.

Of course, our task at hand—Shchukin's and mine—was to help work out a treaty that would usefully limit and cap the strategic offensive and defensive capabilities of the two sides at equal and verifiable levels. At one point, Henry Kissinger and Anatoly Dobrynin, representing Nixon and Brezhnev, attempted to simplify our task by agreeing that we should concentrate on arriving at a definitive ABM treaty while concurrently putting some manner of freeze on the rapid expansion of new starts of additional offensive weapons.

Shchukin and I agreed that the key to an ABM Treaty should be to constrain the deployment of large powerful phased-array ABM radars. These ABM radars are larger than the Egyptian pyramids, take five to ten years to build, and have immense power. They can send out an electronic beam that will hit an object as small as a football three to five thousand miles away. Some small portion of the energy in the beam will bounce back off the surface of such an object and return to approximately the beam's point of origin. A huge receiver near the point of origin will pick up this reflected energy. Complicated electronics can then extract an amazing array of information from this reflected energy. It is thereby possible to determine the position of the object being observed, its velocity, where it is headed, and where it came from, all with phenomenal precision.

Shchukin had supervised the designing of many of the Soviet radars. I was assisted by Charlie Lerch, of the Systems Planning Corporation, who had designed and supervised the building of the first big U.S. phased-array radar. If the sides wished to limit the capability of such radars it was not difficult to agree on the equations relating the factors that determine such a radar's capabilities. Roughly, it is the area of the antenna (measured in square meters) times the average emitted power (measured in watts). Where Shchukin and I differed was on the size of the number of watt-meters squared to be permitted.

The number the Soviet side insisted upon was a thousand times the number Charlie Lerch and I thought should be the maximum permitted if the treaty was to accomplish its intended purpose. But there was also a different and apparently overriding problem. Shchukin's bosses found it impossible to grasp what such a number meant and the Politburo was not about to agree to something they couldn't understand. They suggested using the capabilities of certain then-existing radars as a standard of measurement. The Soviets, however, didn't want to use our radars as the standard and refused to let us inspect and measure the capabilities of theirs. Eventually, they agreed that there was no acceptable way of setting an agreed standard other than to agree on a specific number of watts, times meters squared. The number the sides finally agreed upon was three times ten to the sixth power squared. That esoteric-sounding number remains an essential element of the ABM Treaty to this day.

For me, these discussions and negotiations with Shchukin had an important and lasting impact on the development of my thinking concerning interconnections between logic, mathematics, and the scientific method and political theory, including conflicting value judgments between Soviet doctrine and U.S. and Western political thought.

My own ideas on politics and political theory evolved over the years as I practiced politics and as I taught. Between and following my active periods of participation in U.S. policy formation and implementation, first in the State Department, then in the Pentagon, and finally as an arms control negotiator, I devoted time to teaching and to thinking about how and why political decisions are, or should be, made. Among other thoughts, it became more and more evident to me that no one can act on the complex and important policy issues at the forward edge of emerging history without having formed some rough simplifying approaches to such issues. One needed some set of guidelines. In retrospect, it was not difficult to see where, over the years, errors had been made, where leaders had gotten the cart before the horse, put the narrower value before the more general and greater value, favored short-run public opinion gains against longer-run strategic loss, where I myself had made serious errors of judgment. All this contributed to my determination to put together, and continuously refine, an outline, or framework of thought, concerning a theory of politics.

Why a theory of "politics" rather than a theory of foreign policy, international relations, grand strategy, or some other such characterization? I settled upon "politics" because "foreign policy" suggests a downgrading of economic and military factors and "international relations" presupposes the dominance of nation states. The word "politics" may suggest a focus on government politics or party politics, but the phrases "corporate politics," "family politics," and "personal politics" convey a wider meaning for the term, something encompassing more areas of human interaction. It was for these reasons that I settled on the theory of "politics."

My interest in political theory was stimulated in 1948 when my sister Pussy and her husband Walter Paepcke decided to organize a summer festival in Aspen, Colorado, honoring the two hundredth anniversary of the birth of Goethe, the great German poet, dramatist, and philosopher. Among those who came and gave speeches honoring Goethe were the Belgian musician, philosopher, and doctor Albert Schweitzer, and the Spanish philosopher Ortega y Gasset. They both referred to a well-known passage from Goethe: "The domain assigned to human reason is that of work and action. Being active, reason rarely risks going astray. But what is duty?" Goethe replies: "What the day demands. It is for us to open our eyes to realize our immediate duties and to carry them out. In doing this, we become able to see what tasks remain to be done."[1]

It seemed to me that Goethe had put his finger on the heart of the matter. It is by action—in my terms, by the practice of politics—that theory (in Goethe's terms: one's duty) can be kept in touch with reality. Furthermore, it is by action that one best learns what are the opportunities and risks of the future. The two are inseparable; theory and practice being complementary, they constitute harmonic aspects of one whole. Together they neatly defined what I considered the real subject of political theory.

The interest stimulated at Aspen recalled an earlier, and similar, insight into political theory. When I was doing graduate work at Harvard in 1938, I had prepared a thesis on Oswald Spengler in a sociology course given by Pitrim Sorokin. I found that the Harvard Library had a copy of Spengler's doctoral thesis on the early Greek philosopher Heraclitus. Fewer than thirty fragments from Heraclitus have survived, but his influence on the subsequent evolution of philosophic thought has been profound. One aspect of Heraclitus' thinking that deeply impressed Spengler was his assertion that truth and beauty were to be found in the tension between opposites. To illustrate his point he used the examples of the bow and the lyre. The power of the bow comes from the tension between the two arms of the bow and its directed release; the harmony and beauty of the tones of the lyre come from the varying tensions of its strings.

---

[1] Goethe, *Sprüche in Prosa*, Part III, verse 151.

Some years later, in 1953, I was asked to give the commencement address at Groton School, where my son Peter was a member of the graduating class. I can recall no other speech to which I have devoted as much effort and preparation. Remembering how cruel some of my classmates and I had been to a fellow student whose uncle's sermon—he was the Episcopal Bishop of Connecticut—we had found boring, I was determined not to humiliate Peter or to talk down to his classmates. The heart of the speech went as follows:

This unity of apparent opposites seems to me to involve a basic and crucial point. Twenty-five hundred years ago, Heraclitus, using the analogies of the bow and of the lyre, suggested that harmony and truth were to be found in the tension of opposites. Today advanced modern scientists, such as Robert Oppenheimer and Niels Bohr, apply a parallel idea. They tell us that an undertaking of the basic truths in their field can be attained only by the concurrent application of complementary ideas which to our senses seem contradictory, as for example, we can understand the behavior of light only by perceiving it in two opposite concepts, that of the wave and that of the particle. They call this the principle of complementarity.

Heraclitus and the atomic scientists go on to suggest that this principle of the complementarity of opposites applies not only to the world of physics, but generally, including the world of human affairs.

The great problems with which all of us have been wrestling, and with which each of you will be called upon to wrestle in very concrete terms, include the individual versus society, change versus continuing order, force versus consent, the East versus the West, power versus responsibility. In each case the answer is to be found not in the elimination of one of the opposites or in any basic compromise between them but in striving for a harmony in the tension between opposites.

It is the province of a commencement speaker to give advice. I offer the following.

The first is to strive for both the general and the concrete. Some men combine in themselves a general wisdom derived from a deep background in the humanities and the general sciences with an ability to deal responsibly with particulars. Such men retain breadth of vision with a sense of care for relevant details. They make a wholly disproportionate contribution in the world of affairs. Again it is not a compromise between the general and the concrete which I am advocating. In the field of foreign affairs for instance, it is not those who have taken specialized courses in international affairs who make the real contribution; it is those who combine a truly humanistic background with a sense for relevant facts and an intense care for the significant details who are invaluable.

My second bit of advice would be to head into problems rather than away from them. If one heads into problems, if one addresses oneself to solving problems rather than fighting the fact that there is a problem, if one finds at an early age opportunities to assume responsibilities, then all manner of opportunities open out before one for satisfying service. In order to be able to carry responsibility in important matters, it is essential to have gained experience through trial and error in handling responsibility in smaller matters. It is only after one has survived and overcome a number of failures that one develops the stamina and courage to become a participant and molder of history—not merely an object of history.

My third bit of advice deals with the opposites of humility and of pride. I would apply the advice of Heraclitus and of the modern scientists to these opposites. Both are essential: humility before God, before nature, before mankind; pride in one's faith, in one's country and in one's association with one's fellow man. Only with humility can men gain wisdom and a true sense of relationship with God and with mankind. But only with a due sense of pride in oneself, in one's background and in one's country can one act with courage and effectiveness.[2]

Having suggested the tensions of opposites as an important aspect of political theory, let me turn to the tasks of such a theory.[3]

One of the first tasks of a general theory of politics is to select a relatively small number of abstract concepts that bear some continuing relationships one to another. An understanding of these relationships will help us evaluate the complex data found in the concrete world of action, the practical everyday world.

In creating a general theory, there is a presumption in favor of a more elegant, or simple, approach than of a more complex one.

[2]   The complete text of the Groton commencement address (1953) was published in *Paul H. Nitze on Foreign Policy* (Lanham, MD: University Press of America, 1989), pp. 5–9.

[3]   Many of my thoughts on the elements of a general theory of politics were first published as a chapter in William T. R. Fox's *Theoretical Aspects of International Relations* (Notre Dame, IN: University of Notre Dame Press, 1959). These were also reprinted in *Paul H. Nitze on Foreign Policy,* cited above.

On general grounds, a three- or four-element approach is preferable to a hundred-element approach. But we must ask whether a given theory of politics includes a sufficient number of interacting elements to bear a meaningful relationship to the data they are meant to illuminate. Do its elements in conjunction constitute a necessary and sufficient foundation for a useful theory?

I find that four principal elements are essential to a useful theory of politics. One is the *political structure* of the world whose politics are being considered. Is it dominated by city-states, as was the Greek world about which Thucydides wrote so cogently? Is it a world dominated by tribes? Is it a world increasingly dominated by nation-states, as was the European world after the conclusion of the Thirty Years' War and the Peace of Westphalia? In other words, in a given era, what are the principal political groups of which large numbers of people consider themselves to be members, and thus part of a common "we"? In that context, what are the other groups from which the "we" groups consider themselves to be separated; that is, groups to which the pronoun "they" is more applicable than the pronoun "we"?

The second principal element is the concept of *value system*, or more succinctly, "purpose." What are the values that members of a "we" group share, giving it a collective sense of identity and of purpose? If we examine the attitudes of any identifiable group—the people of the United States, for example—we find thought patterns characteristic of that group's beliefs. Most of them know of and admire leading American athletes in football, basketball, baseball. Most of them have some sense of American values and political history and wish in some way to be part of the team. Some are alienated and wish to bring down the political structure. But, nevertheless, it makes sense to talk about common American values.

A third fundamental category is *situation*. Any analysis of politics requires one to consider the facts of the "situation" in which the political events are assumed to take place. The set of facts that are relevant in a given instance may vary widely. They may include facts of geography, demography, the state of scientific knowledge, the stage of economic development, or the availability of natural resources. They may also include the power of given weapon systems, the origins and the substance of the political, economic, or military ideas of one's friends, and, more importantly, of one's adversaries, the relevant alliance structures, and the state of public opinion at home and abroad.

Sometimes a problem arises in defining what separates a fact of "structure" from a fact of "situation." The problem is analogous to the situation of deciding which mathematical quantities are to be treated as variables and which as parameters: those variables we can influence and those we cannot. The answer depends upon the field of interest of the observer.

For the student of politics, "structure" and "purpose" are at the center of the field of study and are generally to be treated as variables, while climate, geography, location, resources, or demography, for instance, are generally treated as parameters. These latter factors can change and modify the more important relationships at issue, but they do not form the primary focus of political theory. The observer can usually assume that these parameters have some reasonable, objectively determinable, and constant significance. Thus, the more interesting relations, the variables of political structure—those that can be affected by the politically motivated action of the participants—can be explored with greater concentration and care.

A fourth necessary category in a theory of politics is *viewpoint*: from whose point of view are politics observed? A general theory of politics must be broad enough to permit one to observe a relevant political structure and political action as it evolves from a multiplicity of viewpoints or perspectives. These viewpoints can range from that of a responsible or participating member of a particular group at a particular time, to one that approximates that of a hypothetical observer from Mars studying the emergent characteristics of an interacting system of many cultures, races, states, and classes on earth over the full course of history. The more viewpoints or perspectives an observer uses, the better his understanding of a structure, situation, or purpose, and the better prepared he is to take these other viewpoints into consideration as he makes decisions. Throughout this book, I strive to leave open the full range of possible observer locations or viewpoints.

Taken together, these four abstract, interacting elements form a simple yet useful structure upon which we can build a theory of politics. The problem remains in applying these abstractions to the world of practice. Having removed layers of contingent detail to arrive at the simple essentials of a useful theory that provides insight, we now must reverse the process and add relevant detail before we have something applicable to concrete human affairs. The final decision to take one course of action rather than another is based on human judgments that involve a host of considerations. These judgments are based in part upon rational intellectual process, evaluating facts. But to a large measure they also reflect the character of the individual, the nation, and the society that makes them.

2

POLITICAL THEORY
AND VALUE SYSTEMS

I t is in the world of universities, scholars, scientists, laboratories, and think tanks where political theory is studied, analyzed, and occasionally created. When I was not engaged in business or government, either as a staff officer or as a responsible line officer, I was associated, in one way or another, with the classroom. My most important academic connection has been with The Johns Hopkins University School of Advanced International Studies (SAIS) in Washington, D.C.

SAIS got its start during the summer and fall of 1943 as a result of a series of long discussions with Christian A. Herter. At that time Chris was a Republican congressman from Massachusetts and I was working for Henry Wallace in the Board of Economic Warfare (BEW). What had originally brought us together was that our wives were not only first cousins but close friends. Both families had summer houses on Long Island Sound close to Glen Cove; in the spring the Nitzes often went quail shooting at the Herters' plantation in South Carolina; in June or July the Herters would go salmon fishing with us on the Upsalquitch River in New Brunswick. Chris was elected to Congress from a district in Boston on the Republican ticket in 1942. When he moved to Washington, he immediately became an active participant in the Washington wartime policymaking scene.

In 1944, the Dumbarton Oaks conference, which led to the founding of the United Nations and its affiliated agencies, was getting under way. Chris and I became convinced during those days that Hitler would be defeated, that the United States would then face a new and different world, and that its people would be called upon to play a far more important role in the world than they had in the past. To handle this enhanced role with wisdom and character would require that a significant segment of the American people have a better understanding of the world.

During the war, both Chris and I witnessed the practical exposure to the diverse worlds of North Africa, India, South Asia, Latin America, the Western Pacific, and Europe that hundreds of thousands of Americans, both in uniform and as civilians, received as part of their wartime work. What would happen to all that practical experience when the war was over? Would all these people return to their prewar occupations or something similar? Was there anything that could be done to retain, augment, and refine that wisdom to help the United States as a nation carry out its necessary postwar tasks more ably and wisely than we as a nation had done in the years between the world wars?

Chris and I decided an educational institution in Washington was important among the things needed after the war, one that would teach postgraduate students languages, international law, international economics, the cultures of other parts of the world, and the arts of diplomacy and of negotiation. Such an institution should be organized cooperatively by representatives of business, labor, and academia. It should tap the expertise of people working in the government. Its graduates should fan out, compete for admission to the State Department's Foreign Service, for jobs with American businesses and the international agencies or wherever they might be needed.

I was too busy running my part of BEW to have much time to help Chris organize and get the project under way; I had the very immediate task of procuring from foreign sources the strategic materials needed for the Allied war effort. Therefore, the bulk of the effort to create and find support for the school fell to Chris. Chris became president, I treasurer, of the Foreign Service Educational Foundation, which was the vehicle through which the new school was to be financed. Subsequently, Chris went back to Boston, and in 1952 successfully ran for Governor of Massachusetts. He resigned as President of the Foreign Service Educational Foundation. His departure more or less coincided with the termination of my work as director of the State Department Policy Planning Staff, so I agreed to take his place.

I wanted the school to create a research center that would become a source of strategic thought and policy formation in Washington, drawing on and stimulating that portion of the school's faculty more directly responsible for carrying the teaching load. I asked my academic and foundation friends to recommend the leading scholars and teachers of the day in the study of international relations. They told me that two professors, both at the University of Chicago, were outstanding. One was Hans Morgenthau, who had written the textbook most teachers in the field were using. The other was George Liska, a political theorist of Czech origin, who had served during the immediate postwar years in the Czech Ministry of Foreign Affairs, and who was passionately interested in his subject area. I went out to Chicago, talked to them at length, and persuaded them to leave the university there and join the center.

I soon found I had made a mistake in my choice of Morgenthau. He was correct in attempting to oppose the idealistic one-worlders and United Nations enthusiasts with a complementary counteremphasis on realism. But he was vain and self-centered, and his theory that all nations seek only the maximization of that nation's power was patently fallacious. I also found him difficult to work with. To my great relief, he soon left the school. I thus learned the hard way that prestige in the academic world is not synonymous with character or intellectual integrity; one needs to dig deeper.

Eventually, I did find two additional scholars in the foreign policy field whom I admired enormously and persuaded to join our research center. One was Arnold Wolfers, who had taught for years in Germany and Switzerland. After the war he joined Yale University, where he was Sterling Professor of International Affairs and headed one of the Yale Houses whose members specialized in that field. Arnold gave our Foreign Policy Center a sense of direction and recruited an outstanding and varied group of researchers. With their help the center produced excellent and original work in the policy area.

The other scholar was Arnold Brecht, Professor Emeritus at the New School for Social Research in New York City. He had published a book entitled *Political Theory—The Foundations of Twentieth Century Political Thought*.[1] I found it calm, carefully put together, and tightly reasoned. He thoroughly punctured the hypothesis that political science or sociology rested on anything consistent with the repeatable experiments called for by the scientific method. In one of his chapters he catalogues the wide variety of possible objectives that various German political

---

[1]　Brecht, Arnold, *Political Theory: The Foundations of Twentieth Century Political Thought* (Princeton: Princeton University Press, 1959).

scientists had put forward as being the principal objective of politics and therefore the *summum bonum* from which a structure of political precepts could be deductively derived. That catalogue convincingly demonstrated that positing a single supreme good inescapably leads to gross oversimplification in conflict with reality; a more complex approach with a number of interrelated objectives appeared to be required.

Over the years we brought many talented and experienced people from diverse backgrounds into SAIS and the research center there. Among them was C. B. Marshall, who was a professor of American foreign policy at SAIS from 1966 to 1975 and acting director of the Washington Center from 1970 to 1971. Burt had worked with me on the Policy Planning Staff, joining it in 1950 after Dean Acheson replaced General Marshall as Secretary of State.

Burt grew up in El Paso, where for several years he worked as a reporter. There he spent three years at college before finishing his final year at the University of Texas at Austin. He got into the Harvard Ph.D. program by good luck in hard times and received his degree in 1939. During the war, Burt obtained a direct commission in the Army, ending up as a lieutenant colonel in the Transportation Corps assigned to Washington. Later he was deputy port commander in Manila. After the war, one of his professors and friends at Harvard, "Wild" Bill Elliot, brought Burt to Washington as an assistant on the staff of the House Foreign Affairs Committee, where he worked until he came to the Policy Planning Staff.

Burt's toughmindedness, knowledge of the Army, and his unusual refinement in dealing with ethical and political matters made him invaluable to the planning staff. Over the years I found his creative approaches to problems and his clarity re-

freshing and insightful. While still a member of the Policy
Planning Staff, he gave a series of lectures on foreign policy
at Hollins College. In these lectures Burt displayed his
deep wisdom and his gift for expressing himself, so much so
that the college arranged that they be published in a small
book, *The Limits of Foreign Policy*.[2] What he offered remains
useful and practical to anyone interested in the conduct of foreign policy.

As the title of the book implies, Burt addresses the miscon-
ception among many people about the extent of action possible
in American foreign policy. He notes that the sweep of its problems makes foreign policy especially attractive for those with a
passion for reform, while its complexities and subtleties are rich
with opportunities for generalizers and obsfuscators.[3] He warns
that we should understand that there are practical obstacles and
limits to the conduct of policy, and that to avoid frustration and
disappointment one must not have excessive or idealistic expectations.

For example, Burt points out that there is a common tendency
to exaggerate the power of one's own country in the world and
how much it can affect the actions of other countries. Furthermore, many people put faith in the power of Congress to legis-
late the behavior of other countries, over which, by definition, it
has no authority. Even the appearance of military victory is tran-
sitory, unless like the Romans at Carthage, the victors obliterate
the vanquished—something that Americans decline to do.[4]

---

[2]   Marshall, Charles Burton, *The Limits of Foreign Policy*, (New York:
Henry Holt and Company, 1954).

[3]   ibid., p. 12.

[4]   ibid., p. 22.

Above all, foreign policy is chancy since it attempts to cope both with the future and foreign events. Instead, Burt observes, utility, not perfection, is the test of planning foreign policy, and utility is a modest virtue.[5] He illustrated his point with an example drawn from the Napoleonic Wars. The Duke of Wellington once referred to the differences in concept and planning between his adversary and himself in the Peninsular War. The French plans, he said, were made with a logical perfection and completeness. He likened them to a fine leather harness—admirable and useful until some part were to break, rendering the whole useless. His own plans, he said, were made on the principle of a rope, and as portions broke under the stress of circumstance, he would just tie knots and go on. A foreign policy should be planned on that principle.[6]

The goal of foreign policy is essential, but it is the easy part. "The hard part is deciding what to do in circumstances when one can only do part of what one may wish to do."[7]

A nation's goals inevitably exceed available means, and means have costs. However, the limits of foreign policy are determined not only by our intrinsic capability, but by our steadfastness in shouldering the burden. That, says Marshall, rather than the righteousness of our unexecuted wishes, will be the test of the United States as a great nation.[8]

Such people as Burt, who combined practical political experience with wisdom and insight into the broader scope of problems of policy, helped make SAIS a stimulating place to work

[5] ibid., p. 27.
[6] ibid., p. 27.
[7] ibid., p. 30.
[8] ibid., p. 34.

and teach. They provided a necessary bridge of understanding between theory and policy.

The Foreign Policy Center at SAIS provided me an opportunity to develop further some of my own ideas. An example was a report for Senator William Fulbright prepared by the center. During the Eisenhower Administration, Bill Fulbright was chairman of the Senate Foreign Relations Committee. I had gotten to know him well through Dorothy Dillon, the daughter of my former boss, Clarence Dillon. After I was pushed out by the Eisenhower Administration, I became for a time Senator Fulbright's closest advisor on basic foreign policy issues. At one point, he expressed an interest in the future impact of science and technology on foreign policy. I suggested that his committee contract with our Foreign Policy Center under Arnold Wolfers for a study on that subject.

I drafted one of the chapters of the study we finally submitted to Fulbright. In it we developed—I believe for the first time-the concept of "crisis stability." It explained stability in terms of a ball and a cup. If one puts a ball in a cup and shakes the cup from side to side, the ball will climb up one side and then the other but will tend to return to the bottom of the cup once the shaking has ceased. If on the other hand the ball is put on the top of a cup that is turned upside down, then given a shake, the ball will fly off into space or fall to the ground. The ball in the upright cup is in a position of inherent stability; if disturbed it tends to return to its former position. The ball on the top of the overturned cup is in a position of inherent instability; if disturbed it reacts in a radical and uncontrolled way.

I used that analogy in the chapter to make a point about the inherent instability of the military relationships among the principal European powers in 1914. The understanding that a long war would be disastrous for all the participants dominated pre-World War I military strategy. Meaningful victory for the Germans depended on their ability to force a French surrender before Russia could mobilize her enormous but sluggish military forces. The Germans had the advantage of interior lines and had developed a superior railroad network. Their strategic plan, the Schlieffen Plan, called for a rapid thrust through Belgium to Paris, encircling the French forces to the east. The French and Russians could hope to frustrate the German plan only if their mobilization plans were executed with dispatch and efficiency.

The instability caused by these interacting mobilization plans became critical when a Serbian terrorist murdered the Austrian Archduke at Sarajevo. Austria delivered an ultimatum to the Serbs, who rejected it with Russian support. In response, the Austrians began their mobilization, to which the Russians decided they must promptly respond. The Germans then concluded they could not delay their own mobilization and the French followed. Once the process of competitive mobilization had begun it could no longer be controlled by the politicians, and some may not have wanted to control it. I drew from this example the precept that, in the nuclear age, everything possible must be done to avoid what I called "crisis instability," a situation that would offer a significant inherent advantage to the side that could strike the first nuclear blow in a serious crisis threatening war.

In the course of working on the study for Bill Fulbright, I had extended discussions with a research assistant, Ernest Lefever, who later became head of the Ethics and Public Policy Institute. Through Ernest I met Reinhold Niebuhr and later Father John Courtney Murray, the director of the Jesuit Theological Seminary at Woodstock, Maryland. With these two men I had the opportunity to discuss the serious problems of foreign policy and of politics in general that kept arising at the moving edge of emerging history. Their thoughts helped me develop a framework of thought to better grapple with these problems.

I developed a particularly close friendship with Father Murray. He would often spend some days at Loyola, the Jesuit retreat just south of our farm on the Potomac River, and on occasion he would stay with us for a day or two after his retreat. His was a profound and clear mind. I believe he enjoyed being exposed to the concrete current problems of international affairs and joining with me in exploring the political, ethical, and philosophical aspects of the judgments that needed to be made about these issues.

Unfortunately, my discussions with Father Murray were cut short. The Pope was organizing an Ecumenical Council to conduct a comprehensive review of Catholic doctrine and to assess the church's role in the modern world. He ordered Father Murray to leave his theological seminary in Maryland and move to Rome where he would become the executive secretary of the council. He didn't return to Washington for seven years. I thus lost my wisest and most profound advisor.

During this period, I also met Dr. William Loos, the executive director of the Council on Religion and International Affairs (CRIA). Dr. Loos asked me to write an article on ethics and foreign policy for his organization. It was published under the title *The Recovery of Ethics.*[9]

In it I gave more life and detail to the four basic elements of the theory of politics I outlined in Chapter I. I added my

---

[9] Nitze, Paul H., *The Recovery of Ethics* (New York: Council on Religion and International Affairs, 1960). The article also appears in *Paul H. Nitze on Foreign Policy.*

thoughts on the place of values and moral philosophy in political theory. I also emphasized the need to place the values of individuals and groups within an irreducible ethical framework, upon which one might try to resolve conflicts between opposing values. But my approach to a theory of politics and the place of values and moral philosophy within it have evolved further since *The Recovery of Ethics* appeared in 1960.

One can use a variety of "viewpoints" as starting points to analyze and better understand the politics of past or present events. Using the viewpoints of observers from the relevant times, one can examine and contrast the more interesting and striking elements of "structure," "value system," and "situation" in various historical eras. From the viewpoint of Homer, living in the time of the ancient Dorian migration, around 1200 B.C. to 1000 B.C., the leading political features of the relevant political structure are the Dorian tribes coming down into Greece from the north and establishing a number of kingdoms. Their leaders' "values" or purposes were dominated by a striving for personal honor, and the jealousies, friendships, and loves of individual outstanding warriors. If one is examining the time of the Peloponnesian Wars from the viewpoint of Thucydides and his contemporaries in the fifth century B.C., the Greek city-states led by Athens and Sparta are the primary entities of the relevant political structure.

Similarly, if one takes the viewpoint of an observer during the life span of Polybius, examining the political structure some five hundred years after the Peloponnesian Wars, one finds that the central development of that era was the consolidation of Roman power over the entire Greco-Roman world. When Polybius was born, Rome was a minor city-state in the center of the Italian peninsula; by the time of his death, Rome dominated the Mediterranean world. The "values" and purposes of that time focused on the state, public office, and position. If one were to take the viewpoint of Machiavelli or another Italian of the fifteenth and sixteenth centuries, the relevant "structures" would be small states, influential families, and the Church. Their "values" would be a mix of strong religious values, new ideas of commerce and economics, and the beginnings of a renewed belief in the perfectibility of man.

A long-term view of "structure" from these various historical viewpoints reveals a more encompassing and sophisticated definition of political structure, one with a variety of overlapping group structures of which an individual is, or may be, a part. These include the family, the tribe, the nation, the state, and the empire. Depending on time and circumstance, common race or common religion may provide even more binding group ties than state or nation. In the case of dedicated Marxist-Leninists, loyalty to party has taken precedence over all other ties including family, tribe, race, nation or religion.

Often those groups or states that claim sovereignty or a monopoly on the use of legitimate use of force in a given area may also have a particular significance. Serious political problems, even revolution and war, are often associated with conflicts over the legitimacy and geographic reach of claims to sovereignty of states. Apart from the conflicts between states over sovereignty there can be challenges to the legitimacy of a group or national sovereignty within those states. Some viewpoints will see religious groups and groups based on a particular ideology as counter-nationalist or subversive, dedicated to undermining the authority of the government claiming a monopoly on the legitimate use of force. These groups viewed by nationalists as subversive may include people from the Catholic, Protestant, Jewish, Muslim, Hindu, Buddhist, or Confucian traditions, the Fascists, the Marxist-Leninist Communists, and the anarchists, wherever they exist in the world.

In addition to formal groups, such as city, state and nation, church and ideology, there are informal groupings that play significant roles in the theory and practice of politics. These include class and party, as well as elites, caste, functional groups, social groups, corporations, and clubs, among others. Related to these identifications or associations is a consideration of the status and role of individuals in a range of social and political contexts.

Yet another category of more abstract organized "structures" or entities of interest to the student of politics are political, social and cultural institutions. These include the purely political institutions such as executive, legislative, judicial, constitutions, and elections, as well as social and political beliefs such as law, custom, and tradition. Social and economic institutions such as public opinion, pressure groups, functional nongovernmental institutions such as Chambers of Commerce, the Atlantic Council, the AFL-CIO, the World Council of Churches, or the Audubon Society also play an important part.

At levels closer to the individual we find groups and organizations more immediately and directly involved with their individual members. These include not only business organizations such as banks, industrial corporations, and law firms, but also universities, schools, churches, organized charities, and groups lobbying for every conceivable aggregation of people having special interests in common.

In considering any given political question, after having done one's best objectively to understand and specify the relevant political structure, it is useful to identify the points in that political structure from which one wishes to examine the question. Generally, the most significant points are the principal actors; those individuals or groups whose decisions bear most directly on the possible outcomes of the action. To understand these individuals or groups requires understanding what motivates them—their purpose.

Each individual and each group has a characteristic set of beliefs, or values, which guide his or the group's sense of what it should, or should not, do or approve of in the actions of others. These values tend to sort themselves into a hierarchical structure of values ordered in accordance with their relative positive or negative weight. Such a hierarchy of values associated with the full structure of interrelated social groups as they impinge upon the individuals or groups being observed at a given time can be referred to as a "value system." A distinction needs to be made between value systems that have grown naturally among the members of a political entity over the course of succeeding generations, and an ideology set forth by a great charismatic leader. The former is an organic growth, the latter is virtually complete as originally formulated.

For a sociologist, the intensity of the psychological hold that a given value system has on its individual members and subordinate groups is of major significance. Sociologists find that there are factors that lead to, or are indicative of, the intensity of such psychological hold. These factors include the scope of the value system: Does it cover the full range of value issues on which the relevant individual members and subgroups sense the need for group guidance and support? Does it have internal consistency or does it contain anomalies and internal contradictions? Does it have claims to legitimacy? How broadly do its members support and participate in actions taken in the group's name? Is the value system relevant to the current problems, challenges, and hopes of the time in which the group finds itself? The answers to these questions will bear on the intensity of the group's psychological hold on the individuals adhering to the group.

There are indicators of insufficient or of excessive hold of value systems. "Anomie" is the term used by French sociologist Emile Durkheim to describe insufficient support from the society's structure and value system for the mental health of its individuals. A common case in the United States today is a child of a mother with no husband, with little education, little skill, who can find little support in the society in which he is born. At the opposite end of the spectrum is the situation in which the rules or standards of the group in which the individual is brought up are so strict and difficult to implement as to cause him intense self-criticism and even despair. Durkheim describes this situation as "excessive compulsion."

In extreme cases of either "anomie" or "excessive compulsion" demographic statistics indicate an abnormal and sharp rise in suicide rates. Durkheim refers to extreme cases such as dedicated Jesuit priests and Japanese prewar Army officers whose suicide rates were exceptionally high. More recent examples might include the followers of Reverend Jim Jones, who in 1978 followed their cult leader into death in the Guyana jungle, or heiress Patty Hearst's conversion from captive of to collaborator with the Symbionese Liberation Army, and her involvement in their war on society in the 1970s.

Vilfredo Pareto, the Italian sociologist, and others, have studied the distinction between what politicians say about the reasons for their actions, which Pareto called "derivatives," and the true reasons therefor, which he called "residues."[10] Most cultures have developed non-rational modes, as well as reasoned modes, to express and to reinforce their value systems. The role and

[10]   Pareto, Vilfredo, *The Mind and Society: Vol. III Theory of Derivations* (New York: Harcourt, Brace & Co., 1935).

function of these non-rational elements of a culture may provide the glue that holds the group together. They, therefore, merit a place in a theory of politics.

When examining a particular value system, one should identify for whom and against whom its values are directed. Are they oriented to promote the interests of the "I" or of one or more of the interrelated "we" groups, whose values he, or "they" shares? What are the excluded or opposed "they" groups? In view of the fact that the individual is generally a member of a hierarchy of interlocking groups, conflicts of loyalties between his attachments to those several groups are bound to arise. Such conflicts of loyalty are among the most basic issues of politics.

Generally, the main drive of a group's value system, its "purpose," is related to the survival and the well-being of the group, which is generally challenged by the active or passive opposition of various "they" groups. Associated with the group's "purpose" one finds ends which are deemed desirable and approved actions consistent with those ends. A group's value system generally also specifies actions or means which should not, or must not, be used even in pursuit of desirable ends. The means/ends interrelations in the value system thus become a hierarchical structure covering the use of appropriate means to achieve desired and approved ends and the non-use of disapproved means: ethical constraints.

The relationship of means to ends, the degree to which actions or means are restrained in pursuit of an end, is determined in part by the place to be given to preserving "diversity" in a means/ends hierarchy of values. In a U.S., or more generally in a "liberal" value system, diversity has a high position. The means used to achieve ends, and their effect on diversity, their costs, are carefully considered. In a totalitarian value system, or what totalitarians are apt to call "doctrine," diversity has either no position or a minor position to be dealt with under "the theory of contradiction." In such systems means are defined by ends, and are seen as necessary to achieve those desired ends.

Increasing the power of the "we" group versus the power or potential power of the "they" groups is in a somewhat different position than other ends in a value system. Looked at from the top of an ends/means hierarchy of values, power is a necessary means to the achievement of desirable values. Looked at from lower down in the hierarchy, increasing the relative power of the "we" group can appear to be an end in itself. Sorting out the ethical and pragmatic considerations involved in resolving these issues is one of the most difficult tasks both in devising a comprehensive theory of politics and in the practice of politics.

As an aid to resolving the problems and issues outlined above, political actors and political theorists have attempted to work out sets of principles as guides to the choice of means and to limitations on their use. These can be useful, but the task of arriving at a set of irreducible ethical or moral principles upon which to guide political action (reconciling means and ends) and concurrently to resolve the conflicts between value systems presents an unending challenge and task.

A central, and most complex, problem in thought about the practice and theory of politics is that of arriving at a judgment as to whether one value system is objectively "better" than another. By what criteria should the relative objective excellence of differing value systems be compared and judged? It is difficult to be impartial about one's own value system. But when one examines the value systems of other political entities and cultures as they developed, evolved, and sometimes ended over the course of history, it may be possible to derive from that examination criteria to aid in judging the relative objective merit of specific value systems, including one's own.

A common method is to compare specific values with those held by one's parents, grandparents and their ancestors; in other words, by tradition. In an era of rapid change such as that of today, value problems are often quite different from those faced in times past and to which past value systems were relevant. There is reason to presume that ancestral values had merit in their context, but one should be willing to move forward when persuaded that traditional values are no longer sufficiently applicable and that the value system needs to be modified better to fit the new objective realities.

Some political theorists, such as Arnold Toynbee, suggest that the proper criterion to be used in evaluating a value system is the extent to which it can or has contributed to the survival of the political entities which adhere to it. But a review of the history of political entities, their value systems, and the length of their survival leads to serious doubt that this criterion can be considered absolute. Sparta had a unique political structure and value system which persisted relatively unchanged for some six hundred years. Athens' system continued unchanged for a lesser period. But is it justified to place Sparta's value system on a higher plane than that of Athens? Athens provided far greater scope for creativity, beauty, and the full development of the potentialities of the human mind and spirit. Thus mere persistence does not appear to be an adequate objective criterion; brutal tyrannies have persisted for centuries.

The student of a theory of politics is thus forced to look to the more basic sources of belief; to examine religion, ideology, or criteria derived from philosophy, such as ethics, moral order, and natural law. Because of the exclusivity of most religions and ideologies, they do not lend themselves easily to providing objective values for a comprehensive theory of politics providing general insights applicable across the world over broad periods of time in the past and hopefully for the future.

Perhaps the most hopeful approach is the careful and comprehensive study of history, winnowing out and eliminating those value systems that have in the past encouraged repellent results and then attempting to find systems of values that promise to encourage or produce more generally satisfactory results. From such an approach the direction in which to search for an optimum value system for the future can emerge. This is analogous to what has happened in the evolution of the physical sciences.

In mathematics and the physical sciences progress has been made by intermittent but occasionally giant steps. Radically new steps such as the Newtonian approach to gravity and to mechanics swept away much of past guessing about the motion of celestial objects. Then Einstein's General Theory of Relativity and the almost concurrent development of quantum mechanics swept away much of Newtonian mechanics. But it did so only at the margins of the extremely big or the minutely small. In the realm of immediate interest to the common man nothing much appeared to have changed. Similarly, the evolution of thinking about politics may make some recent thinking and writing about politics obsolete while revalidating much of the common wisdom accumulated over the centuries.

3

TOWARD AN ETHICAL
FRAMEWORK

The foundation of political theory and political action, or practice, must provide a profound and consistent basis from which one can derive guidance and reach ethical judgments. The source of this foundation is still debated among theorists and practitioners, for its form shapes political outlook, ideology, and ultimately political action. Some political theorists will couch their arguments in discussions of the nature of man as good or evil and the question of the perfectibility of man. Others will approach the problem from an interpretation of the behavior or psychology of man—what motivates him as an individual or group. For them the most elemental of motives is self-preservation.

However, the foundation of political thought and action cannot rest exclusively on values derived from individual self-interest or the survival of existing groups. These values serve only the instinctive interests of self-preservation. They tend to exacerbate rather than resolve political conflict. There is a rich panoply of other and more complex issues in political life: these are the issues which involve moral and ethical judgement. Morality and ethics should stem from a point of view above self-serving motives; they should give point, order, and harmony to the resolution of the manifold political issues arising from diverse groups and their diverse value systems. In short, the foundation of political theory and political practice must be objective, universal, and in part altruistic if it is to offer lasting practical guidance.

The search for a basic ethical framework itself requires objectivity and intellectual rigor. Some twentieth-century developments in modern science and their implications for philosophy may aid us in our search for an ethical approach, even if we can produce no certainties. One such development is the rejection of the blind mechanical determinism that flowed from Newtonian mechanics and that appeared inconsistent with ethically oriented and responsible human will. Once scientists realized that the portion of reality covered by scientific concepts is strictly limited, and that the part not covered by these concepts includes "should" propositions—which suggest value systems—an ethical view of the world not in contradiction with science again became possible.

Similarly, changes in fundamental ideas of philosophy, particularly concepts of ontology, epistemology, and logic, have altered old definitions of truth. Few now believe with the logical positivists that truth is limited to those hypotheses that can be confirmed by repeatable scientific experiments. As our confidence in our complete understanding of the material structure of the universe has declined, our confidence in the concepts and roles of purpose, relation, mediation, probability, and chance has risen. It is now possible to believe that the "reality" of general ideas, such as justice or duty, is on a par with the "reality" of such concepts of nuclear physics as quarks, with their characteristics such as "color" and "strangeness."

These developments have undermined our confidence in the

adequacy of past modes of thought to address the nature and purpose of the world around us, of man, and of life. They have also reawakened our interest in contemplating the fundamentals of human values, a task that no longer convicts one of being a crank. Thinking about politics and ethics in the modern world has advanced to the point where it is possible to make a major step forward toward greater clarity, precision, and understanding. We may be able to create an ethical framework within which we can reach more objective judgments concerning choices among values and value systems.

Perhaps the best point at which to start a search for an ethical framework is to look for the source of human activity. It is evident to anyone who looks about himself with open eyes that living things strive to live and to bring to pass some specific potential inherent in their being. While for many animals a sense of purpose may be nothing more than instinctive, in man at least, the sense of purpose transcends the instinctive—itself a subject of some discussion—into a sense of being.

It is the sense of being and awareness that moves men and allows them to accumulate knowledge of themselves and the world about them. This contributes to his existing, natural sense of purpose. But we know few things for certain (we have already acknowledged the limits of scientifically verifiable reality) and must make informed guesses about the rest of our perceptions based on reason, guidance, and intuition.

Sometimes we accept things we perceive without a full understanding of "why." For instance, I know I can and do think, and I see no reason why other people, and other animate entities, are much different from me in this regard. At the same time, we are told that the very minds with which we think are somehow enmeshed in our brains, composed of billions of cells and neurons, in turn made up of even larger numbers of molecules, themselves of still larger numbers of atoms. Nuclear physicists tell us that those atoms are made up of enormous numbers of subatomic particles and forces of which we know very little. We see the symptoms of their existence and behavior, but do not understand their essence. Likewise, we understand that the cumulative effect of the association of these forces and structures permits us to think—for we do so—but we must simply accept that they do, for we do not understand how.

Just as we accept the limitations of verifiable reality and look beyond them for guidance in our knowledge of the mechanical universe, we also accept the limitations of our experience: what we know about ourselves and our past. For example, we know that the accumulated wisdom and experience of the past do not always give unambiguous precedents for decisions and actions at the relevant margin of freedom that is the present. History repeats itself only broadly. A new integration of general concepts of purpose and direction with the concrete dangers and possibilities of the present then becomes necessary.

We also know from experience that in the short run the human will is effective only at the margin of world events. We can only minimally influence the immediate outcome of events, but the "narrow margin of today" can become the broader possibility of the future. We can and do put incremental change into play, however: an action of a day or so can set a course that over time will have enormous consequences. Even a Lincoln could not free the slaves in a day. When he chose Ulysses Grant to take overall command of his army, he took the step necessary to restore unity to the United States and thus make freeing the slaves possible. Likewise, it took years of superior generalship for the

Duke of Wellington to bring down Napoleon: in his long campaign in Spain, he gained the experience to make possible his victory at Waterloo. Lenin did not create his "dictatorship of the proletariat" overnight, but during a few weeks in October 1917 set a series of events into motion based on the aim of achieving the worldwide triumph of communism which, before it ran out of steam, would almost destroy the world.

Marxist-Leninist doctrine as it evolved over the years is not without ideas that can be helpful in wholly different contexts. One of these is that changes in degree can reach a point where they become changes in kind. When such changes in kind occur, fundamental changes in ideas and policies may become necessary. For more than two hundred and fifty years there was so much uncultivated and unexploited land in the United States that conservation made little sense. But degree by degree the frontier closed in, its land overused, its waters overfished and polluted, its animals slaughtered by the millions, and its forests clear-cut. Eventually, this society reached a point where changes in degree had become a change in kind, where the cumulative effect of separate abuses brought about an acute crisis. Preserving the environment we once took for granted has become a must.

Similarly, we can note, over the last fifty years, a plethora of changes about thinking that has affected the theory and practice of politics. These changes of degree have become changes in kind. The understanding of the limitations of science, and the new approaches to philosophy thus engendered, all developed amid these uncertain, unsteady changes of degree and culminated in a profound change of kind. We may again accept the possibility of truths and begin to look for them. This leads to the conclusion that the development of an ethical framework more deeply and objectively based than the largely self-oriented value systems of a particular individual and his associated groups may now be possible. A number of people have attempted to make such a breakthrough in thought and analysis. I believe an important step forward was made by the great British lawyer and politician, Quintin Hogg, later Lord Hailsham.

Hailsham was born some eight years before the outbreak of World War I. He was educated at Eton and then Christ Church College at Oxford, studying primarily the Latin and Greek languages and culture and graduating with honors in 1928. He describes his education as filled with moral content based largely on classical examples.

In his book *The Door Wherein I Went*, Hailsham argues that there is a natural morality—one inherent in human nature—that is expressed in general guidelines such as "tell the truth," "honor thy mother," "love your country," "do not murder, steal, or lie." As they are but guidelines, there are exceptions that are hard to express or limit.[1] But we accept these guidelines as truths that, if observed, make life better. Such natural morality stems from a concern with how to act, not how *not* to act—emphasizing the positive or good over the negative or bad.

Hailsham uses the words "nature" and "natural" to describe value judgments to which one can come unassisted by divine revelation or by the authoritative pronouncements of any particular group. He believes that once you have accepted that observation, measurement, and verification are not the only marks of

---

[1] Hogg, Quintin (Lord Hailsham), *The Door Wherein I Went* (London: Collins, 1975), p. 20.

significant truth, you need not worry that assessments of value do not necessarily involve these elements.

Hailsham carries his concept of natural morality over to the law and to political life where he finds it tempers our sense of justice and decency. He points out that ". . .the purely formal definition of law stated by the nineteenth-century writers on jurisprudence, 'Law is the command of the ruler,' is, in fact, indistinguishable from Hitler's definition 'Das ist Recht was dem Führer gefällt.'" Instead, one may interfere with the freedom of another only when it is "arguable that that other is already under some obligation to do or to refrain from doing the sort of thing that a proposed law imposes as a duty under penalty or prohibits." Obviously, this does not mean that all moral duties ought to be enforced by law. "It only means that there must be a relationship of some kind between law and morality, however much the relationship is tempered by the need for freedom (itself a moral concept) or by practical considerations of common sense."[2] Thus, in Hailsham's view of morality and ethics, a natural morality underlies political activity as a source of guidance and justice at all levels.

Isaiah Berlin has, over the years, come to somewhat similar conclusions about the sources and universality of morality and ethics. Born in Latvia, he lived in St. Petersburg through the 1917 October Revolution. In 1919, he went to England, where he was educated at Corpus Christi College, Oxford. In 1942, he came to Washington as part of the staff of the British Embassy. He quickly became one of a group of friends of which I was one. Chip Bohlen, who was in charge of the Eastern European (including Russia) section of the State Department, was perhaps

[2] ibid., p. 21.

the most influential member of the group. It also included Frank Wisner who had dealt with Soviet matters in the OSS, and did so later in the CIA, and Joe and Stewart Alsop who together published one of the most interesting syndicated columns of political comment of the day.

Isaiah, who found a small apartment just off the entrance to Stewart Alsop's house on Rodman Street in Washington, had diverse interests in ideas and values. He had made a careful and insightful study of the development of Russian intellectual ideas during the nineteenth century and also came to understand well both British politics and American politics. After the war, he went back to Oxford and had a most distinguished career as a professor of social and political theory. There he became immersed in the ideas of Ludwig Wittgenstein and the neo-positivists. From time to time he and I exchanged letters on some of the more obscure—and I thought misguided—of his ideas during that period. But eventually he put all that aside and went on to do truly solid work in the realm of ideas and values.

Berlin ascribes his conversion from extreme skepticism of moral values to his study of Tolstoy and the other Russian writers of the mid-nineteenth century. He says their approach seemed to him to be essentially moral and that they sought the sources of

> ...injustice, oppression, falsity in human relations, imprisonment whether by stone walls or conformism—unprotesting submission to man-made yokes—moral blindness, egoism, cruelty, humiliation, servility, poverty, helplessness, bitter indignation, despair, on the part of so many. In short, they were concerned with the nature of

these experiences and their roots in the human condition; the condition of Russia in the first place, but, by implication, of all mankind.[3]

The same authors also sought the solutions to these problems, and to bring about "truth, love, honesty, justice, security, personal relations based on the possibility of human dignity, decency, independence, freedom, spiritual fulfillment."[4]

While at Oxford, Berlin read the works of the great philosophers and found that they shared the belief that solutions to the central problems existed, that we could discover them, and that with sufficient selfless effort we could approximate them. He says this view was at the heart of the critical empiricism that he imbibed as a student in Oxford. He learned to reject the fallacy of final solutions, and to distinguish choice between competing values from morally deadening relativity.

Berlin believes that there is a world of objective values, ends "which men pursue for their own sake."[5] But these values are often in collision. Both liberty and equality, he notes, are "among the primary goals pursued by human beings through the centuries; but total liberty for wolves is death to the lambs."[6] The collision of values, he argues, is who we are. There is no ultimate solution in which all things, or values, exist. However, this should not deter us from seeking a better society. We can "soften" the collision of values. What should

---

[3] Berlin, Isaiah, "On Pursuit of the Ideal," in *The Crooked Timber of Humanity* (New York: A. A. Knopf, 1991), p. 3.

[4] ibid., p. 3.

[5] ibid., p. 11.

[6] ibid., p. 12.

guide our actions is to avoid extremes of suffering, embrace humility, civility, and decency to promote and preserve "an uneasy equilibrium."[7]

Berlin's viewpoint is that of a scholar and philosopher looking out at the world of Western culture and the common values that hold it together. He leaves me in doubt, however, whether "civility" and "decency" are the values he believes to be appropriate to all political action, including dealing wisely with opponents such as Lenin, Hitler, or Saddam Hussein with quite different value systems. My theory of politics, in contrast, holds that to fill out one's understanding of the world of politics one needs to include the concept of a number of "they's," not merely a number of expanding and interrelated "we's." The real world contains not only common interests, but radically opposed ones.

In a brilliant essay on "Joseph de Maistre and the Origins of Fascism,"[8] Berlin found the eloquent stylist and insightful mind that challenged the set of values he absorbed from the Russian authors. A contemporary of the French Revolution from Savoy, de Maistre attacked the basically optimistic views of the Enlightenment culminating around the end of the eighteenth century. Despite differences among individual writers, there were certain beliefs held in common. Enlightenment thinkers generally believed man was by nature rational and sociable, that rules of good conduct and laws governing nature, both animate and inanimate, were discoverable and if widely enough spread would promote harmony among individuals and associations.

Joseph de Maistre assaulted these rational and optimistic

---

[7]   ibid., p. 19.
[8]   ibid., pp. 91–174.

views at their very roots. He held there was no such thing as "man," that there are only men, and that savage man was indeed a brute. He considered most men to need direction, agreeing with Aristotle that they are natural slaves.

De Maistre also insisted that the hierarchy of society is necessary and that discipline must be enforced by the executioner. He argues, notes Berlin, that man "seeks to maximize his pleasures, [and] minimize his pain."[9]

Left to himself he is a self-destructive creature who acts only in his individual interest. To de Maistre, it is society that imposes community and self-sacrifice upon men. The state and the Church, through government, direct men beyond self-aggrandizement, pleasure, and self-interest toward a higher, divine purpose. "Man's first need is that his growing reason be put under the double yoke [of church and state]. It should be annihilated, it should lose itself in the reason of the nation, so that it is transformed from its individual existence into another—communal—being, as a river that falls into the ocean does indeed persist in the midst of the waters, but without name or personal identity."[10]

Berlin observes that the façade of de Maistre's system may be classical, but behind it there is something terrifyingly modern, and violently opposed to sweetness and light.[11] His doctrine is of violence, the power of dark forces, the glorification of chains as alone capable of curbing man's self-destructive instincts, and the belief in using those chains for man's salvation. At the heart of de Maistre's convictions was an appeal to blind faith against rea-

---

[9] ibid., p. 123.

[10] Quoted by Berlin, ibid., p. 126.

[11] ibid., p. 126.

son. Only that which is mysterious can survive, and to explain is always to explain away.[12]

He embraces the doctrine of blood and self-immolation, belief in the national soul and the concept of streams flowing into one vast sea, of the absurdity of liberal individualism, and above all in the subversive influence of uncontrolled critical intellectuals.

Surely we have heard all of this since de Maistre propounded his theories in the eighteenth century. In practice if not in theory, de Maistre's deeply pessimistic vision is the heart of the now discredited totalitarianism—of both left and right—of the twentieth century.

Isaiah Berlin appears to single out de Maistre for special attention because he appears to be more the intellectual forebear of the antirational, extremist, brutal ideologists and tyrants of this century than other thinkers of the early part of the preceding century. His treatment reminds us that a better understanding of evil and its roots is an essential element of understanding politics and, it is hoped, of improving its practice. But I doubt that a writer such as de Maistre who predicts evil while advocating wholly unacceptable measures to head it off is worthy of such special treatment.

Dr. Milton Heifetz, professor at the Boston College Law School, has also been engaged in a search for a universally applicable system of morality and ethics whose basic elements he holds to be found in all religions and moral commentaries.[13]

---

[12]   ibid., p. 127.

[13]   Heifetz, Milton D., *Ethics in Foreign Affairs*, unpublished manuscript, Beverly Hills, CA, 1991. The author wishes to express his thanks to Dr. Heifetz for allowing him to present his views herein and for reviewing this chapter.

The central proposition of the system is based upon a universal desire of mankind to avoid harm. From that single concept Dr. Heifetz derived four principles consistent with the negative of the Golden Rule: that you should not do unto others that which you would not wish them to do unto you. This is a less demanding rule than the Judeo-Christian precept that one should love one's neighbor as oneself and has found much wider support. The concept is found, Heifetz asserts, in Judaism, in the Koran, in historical Christianity, in Buddhism, in Confucius, and in Hinduism.[14]

Heifetz proposes four precepts for behavior applicable worldwide and at all times:

1. Do no harm, which can also be derived from the negative golden rule—do not unto others that which you would not have them do unto you.
2. Freedom—as long as others are not hurt by that freedom.
3. Beneficence—action taken for the good of another person. It may spring from a variety of motives and is distinguished from "benevolence" which specifically refers to the motivation to do good and therefore more in tune with the positive golden rule, i.e., to do to others as you would have others do to you and yours.
4. Duty to help for the common good.

Dr. Heifetz extends these four principles to the conduct of foreign policy. He denies, contrary to almost all other political

---

[14]   ibid., p. 24.

theorists of the past, that the conduct of foreign affairs must be amoral to be successful. Rather, he suggests that morality, properly understood in a secular framework, may be most productive of world harmony and peace. His moral framework mandates prudence, not blind self-sacrifice.[15]

To support his argument, Dr. Heifetz quotes several extreme "realists," classic and modern, who reflect the traditional approach that he condemns. Among them are Thucydides, Machiavelli, and Hobbes. Each of these realists argues that observing morality and ethics in the pursuit of foreign affairs causes only weakness. "According to this tradition," Heifetz quotes Marshall Cohen as saying, "international relations occupies an autonomous realm of power politics exempt from moral judgment and immune to moral restraint."[16]

Dr. Heifetz's ire is particularly strong in his opposition to the views of Reinhold Niebuhr. He says that Niebuhr's concept of morality was an important factor in perpetuating an amoral approach to foreign affairs, as exemplified by Morgenthau and Kennan, who continued to think primarily in terms of self-interest and balance of power. Heifetz argues that Niebuhr based his concept of ethics and its application in policy upon a flawed interpretation of religious morality, in which ". . .unselfishness must remain the criterion of the highest morality."[17]

Heifetz argues that, to the contrary, "unselfishness as the epitome of morality is not an integral component of secular morality and possibly even of theological philosophy. Secular morality and therefore national morality does not demand unlimited un-

---

[15]   ibid., p. 68.
[16]   ibid., p. 67.
[17]   ibid., p. 68.

selfishness, only the obligation to do good as long as it does not demand too great a sacrifice."[18]

Instead, Dr. Heifetz offers his own four moral principles of non-maleficence, freedom, beneficence, and common good. They are applicable, he says, not only to individuals and groups within a secular pluralistic nation, but to foreign affairs as well. He recommends that we accept three concepts as given:

1. Governments are inclined to pursue self-centered interests frequently contrary to the interests of other nations.
2. The community of nations exists not only for the good of all nations but is considered by individual nations to exist primarily for the good of that individual nation.
3. But no nation's right to act vis-à-vis another is unlimited and unqualified.[19]

In his essay, Dr. Heifetz affirms that national sovereignty must be seen as inviolate until formal action to transgress it is authorized through due process—regardless of how one may look at the internal structure of another nation, regardless of how immoral its leadership appears to be, and regardless of the degree of oppression used to establish the governing body. Without due process all physical intervention must be taboo, but sanctions and economic pressure are not prohibited. He speculates that the combined action and agreement between the United Nations and the World Court might fulfill the concept of

---

[18] ibid., p. 68.
[19] ibid., from Chapter II, which is unpaginated.

dispassionate due process. But daunting problems are presented as one tries to further develop objective and testable standards by which cruel and inhuman actions by nations may be compared, standards that can provide a basis for decision in specific cases that interference by other nations is warranted. This dilemma may be solved by establishing a list of inhumane actions to be used as a standard for comparison, against which to evaluate the degree of a nation's inhumanity.

Dr. Heifetz also recommends that his four moral principles used to establish a relationship between states—namely non-maleficence, freedom, beneficence, and common good—be slowly inculcated by exposing policymakers to such concepts, primarily by example within our own legislature and State Department. He also suggests that it is better that we deal with brutal nations through quiet direct negotiations rather than through international law, except as a last resort.

I personally much admired the manner in which Secretary of State George Shultz, during the Reagan administration, succeeded in making human rights a major factor in American foreign policy by following a similar policy. World opinion and the foreign policy of many nations have now moved in the direction of encouraging the international observation of human rights. It is now widely acknowledged that the right of a tyrant to rule through grossly inhuman methods is not limitless; forward-looking world opinion appears to favor developing a basis in international law for collective action and humanitarian intervention against gross violations of human rights.

What forms a common thread of wisdom in the thought of Lord Hailsham, Isaiah Berlin, and Dr. Heifetz is the conclusion that most men are not entirely self-serving. They have a disposition to reach out beyond themselves to help others, and have a sense of obligation to do so, within limits. Part of the problem, as these three men acknowledge, is finding these limits and softening the collision of values. To approach an understanding of those limits with lucidity, I suggest that the framework I developed earlier in this book, particularly in Chapter I, is helpful.

In my framework, the disposition, and willingness, of most men to reach out positively beyond themselves applies to actions affecting other members of the hierarchy of the "we" groups of which the actor feels himself to be a part. Quite other precepts apply to actions intended to affect members of the "they" groups opposing those "we" groups. The heroes of the "we" groups are those who most boldly, unselfishly, and successfully oppose leading members of the "they" groups, generally at great personal risk, even at the risk of their lives.

In Chapter I, I also suggested that in addition to the political structure pertinent to the issues under consideration and the value systems affecting members of the various groups involved, it is important to consider the facts of the situation in which the action takes place. These include geography, demography, the state of scientific and technical knowledge, and stages of economic, military, and political development at home and abroad. In other words, one must consider the common ambient in which the action between the "we" groups and the "they" groups takes place. Finally, I proposed that the fourth necessary category in a comprehensive theory of politics is the viewpoint of the observer attempting to judge the relative merits of the value systems and courses of action available to the actors.

I believe that this set of ideas more comprehensively illuminates what we have learned about the theory and practice of politics in this half century than the suggestions of even the great thinkers on the subject dealt with in this essay. The set should provide a framework of practical guidance that can help the practitioner form consistent, ethical and moral policy.

4

RUSSIA,
THE SOVIET UNION,
AND VALUE SYSTEMS

My uncle Henry (Harry) Nitze was a distinguished geologist. Early in my uncle's career, Czar Nicholas II invited him to undertake a geological survey of the Ural Mountains. He spent some years on the task, learned Russian, and published a number of well-known articles on the subject. As a consequence, his father—my grandfather—Charles Nitze became interested in Russian affairs and was eventually appointed Honorary Consul for Russia in Baltimore. From their influence, I too developed an interest in Russia at an early age and later a love for Russian literature including Chekhov, Tolstoy, Dostoyevsky, Turgenev, and Herzen.

After the October Revolution in 1917, I found it hard to accept Lenin, Trotsky, and their associates as anything other than revolutionary radicals consumed by an almost universal hatred of all elements of culture and humanity as those concepts had evolved over the millennia. It appeared that their hatred was as much dedicated to the destruction of Russian culture as it was to that of Western culture.

Over the years I began to understand that even the full weight of totalitarianism and the ideological campaigns of Lenin,

Stalin, and their successors had not succeeded in completely eliminating the inner fire and spirit of the Russians or of the other nationalities comprising the Soviet empire. In fact, the human will to freedom and virtue seemed to produce individuals in the USSR of extraordinary independence, will, courage, and virtue. The best known examples internationally have been a handful of scientists and intellectuals who have spoken out as dissidents.

For example, the great physicist Andrei D. Sakharov openly broke with the Soviet system. In 1968, a pamphlet by Sakharov, *Reflections on Progress, Coexistence, and Intellectual Freedom*, circulated in Moscow. In it he openly challenged the fundamental tenets of Soviet doctrine.

Sakharov asserted that intellectual freedom is essential to human society—freedom to obtain and distribute information, freedom for open-minded and unfearing debate, and freedom from pressure by officialdom and from prejudices. He held that freedom of thought is a precondition to a scientific, democratic approach to politics, economy, and culture. He called for a multiparty political system in the Soviet Union, the end of censorship, and the completion of de-Stalinization. He also called for the victory of the leftist reform wing in capitalist countries, which could lead to a convergence of capitalist and socialist systems; he also predicted the creation of a world government to oversee total disarmament by the end of the twentieth century.

Eventually, the Nomenklatura exiled Sakharov to Gorky and tried its best to humiliate and to muzzle him. Somehow, he continued to express his disdain for the Soviet Nomenklatura and its methods. Sakharov had such international and domestic prestige that the Soviet establishment dared not eliminate him. When in greatest danger of becoming totally isolated he went on a hunger strike. His wife, Elena Bonner, publicized the fact that he was near death. The Soviet authorities, not wishing to be held responsible for his death, finally gave way and released him. In 1985 Sakharov was again on a hunger strike in an effort to persuade the government to grant his wife permission to go abroad for medical treatment. She was granted the permission and was in the United States for treatment when President Reagan met with Secretary Gorbachev in Geneva in November of that year.

I accompanied President Reagan and Secretary Shultz to Moscow that November and stayed with Arthur Hartman, our ambassador to the Soviet Union, at Spaso House. The ambassador gave a formal dinner for us and for the leading Soviet government and military figures. The guest list also included distinguished Soviet artists, athletes, scientists and public figures, among them Sakharov. On that occasion I had the opportunity to speak directly with him. He impressed me as being a rock of granite. He was not only a great mathematician, physicist, and technical explorer but also a solid believer in intellectual freedom, democratic institutions and eventual peaceful convergence with the West.

The last time I saw Sakharov was at the National Academy of Sciences in Washington. He and Jerome Wiesner, the president of MIT, were the cofounders of an institute to study and foster the implementation of programs supporting continuing Soviet/American interests. U.S. private organizations and Soviet governmental agencies were to contribute the required facilities and funds. Shortly thereafter, Wiesner fell ill and died. Somewhat later Sakharov had a massive heart attack and also died. Sakharov was deeply mourned both in the Soviet Union and in the United States. The rest of us supporting the project were unable to keep it alive after the deaths of these two men.

My friend, the academician Alexander Shchukin, of whom I

spoke earlier, had worked with Sakharov and Igor Tamm on the first Soviet thermonuclear device. He considered Sakharov a radical who had abandoned his basic loyalty to the communist system and that his ideas were politically unsound. Although, like Sakharov, he wished to see radical reforms in the personnel and procedures of the Soviet system, Shchukin was never prepared to go as far as Sakharov. He remained loyal to the interests of the Soviet Union as he saw them; however, he did manage to preserve his individual dedication to truth, to the scientific method, and to humanity.

Unfortunately, the survival of the fire of human spirit in Russia among such people as Sakharov did not ensure that a Russian cultural identity and a Russian value system survived with it. An essential precept of communism anywhere is the elimination of national identity in favor of the internationalism of the proletariat. Communists interpret nationalism as a bourgeois identity that masks the common international—and primary—class identity of the worker. To remove national identity required destroying those sources that preserved nationalistic values and identities, particularly "bourgeois" culture.

Lenin, Stalin, and their successors dedicated themselves to the extirpation of Russian culture. All Russian reading matter was purged or rewritten to support Marxist-Leninist ideas. From children's books to authors such as Chekhov, Pushkin, Tolstoy, and Dostoyevsky, published texts were altered to leave the impression that the authors supported humble submission to czars, tyrants, and dictators. The educational system also contributed to the effort. New texts were purified to eliminate all humanistic content from the old ones in favor of Soviet doctrine. In effect, the written record of Russian culture was systematically eliminated.

Intellectuals or the outspoken in all professions were similarly suppressed. Some of the cultural intelligentsia managed to leave or were thrown out: these included Alexandr Solzhenitsyn, Mstislav Rostropovich, and Anatoly Sharansky. Other individuals, particularly from the generation born before the October Revolution in 1917, such as Sakharov, General Nikolai Detinov, and Marshal Sergei Akhromeyev maintained their integrity, showing immense courage in resisting the system. But by 1992 almost no one was left in Russia who remembered the pre-October Revolution days.

Despite the efforts of Soviet ideologists and authorities, the new Soviet value system imposed on Russia and the rest of the old Russian Empire in place of the prerevolutionary value systems was unsatisfactory and insufficient, even to many of the system's leading figures. An excellent example is found in the person of Yuli Kvitsinsky, the man with whom I spent years of my life in serious negotiations.

In November 1981, Kvitsinsky and I met in Geneva to open the negotiation on the reduction and limitation of Intermediate Range Nuclear Forces (INF) in Europe. He was thirty years my junior, seemed to be a person in his own right, not a mere Soviet bureaucrat, and to have a sense of humor. My first impression was that here was a man with whom it might be possible to make rapid and significant progress.

However, it was difficult to find common negotiating ground with Kvitsinsky or to understand his or the Soviet team's goals. In two sessions we cleared away much of the bureaucratic nonsense that usually took much longer to clear away. On the substance of the issues, however, no progress seemed possible. Kvitsinsky did not seem interested in the probable truth or falsity of any statement of fact I made to him. He seemed to be solely interested in discovering the political purpose of my making such a statement at that time. He had an irritating habit of asking me: "What is your motive in making this statement?" If he had asked: "What is your 'reason' for the statement?" perhaps I would have been less put off.

During the initial few months of negotiations, the U.S. team tried hard and persistently to understand something of the Soviet position on the control of intermediate-range missiles. What did they want and why? What kind of an agreement did they have in mind that would meet their agenda and that also might be acceptable to us? They would raise one area of objections to what we were proposing, then a second level, then a third, then a fourth, a fifth, and finally a sixth and seventh, while offering little to clarify their own position. We wrote a report back to Washington after a few months that we entitled "The Dance of the Seven Veils" to describe the seven layers of obfuscation we had had to peel away one by one before we could perceive even a dim outline of what they might have in mind.

We decided to keep up-to-date a looseleaf book entitled the "Issues Book." In it we established a separate section dedicated to each identifiable issue that arose in our discussion with our Soviet partners. Each member of our delegation was under instruction to dictate a memorandum of conversation after each talk he had with a member of the Soviet team.

From the record of formal meetings of the two delegations and these memoranda of conversation it was possible to put together a detailed record of everything that had been said on a given issue by either side during the entire course of the negotiations. From it we could sort out which were the crucial boulders blocking the path to an agreement and which were the secondary rocks that would need to be dealt with when the removal of the boulders had opened a way to consider them. Only then would it become worthwhile to think about the host of less significant issues—what appeared to be the pebbles—hidden behind the secondary rocks.

After studying the "Issues Book" as it grew in size during the initial few months, it became evident that there were four large boulders, perhaps thirty-five secondary rocks and a host of pebbles behind them. Later in the negotiation we worked out with our Soviet counterparts acceptable ways to eliminate the four boulders, but Kvitsinsky was of no help in doing so.

I tried to find out from Kvitsinsky who in Moscow he looked to for his personal political backing. Originally he suggested it was his foreign minister Gromyko. But later he indicated that the situation was more complicated; there were cliques within the ministry. His principal supporter there appeared to be Viktor Komplectov, who dealt with American affairs in the ministry. Later, his support appeared to come from Valentin Falin, who specialized in German political affairs. However, Falin remarried and his new wife had a son who had said or done things that were not acceptable to others high in the Soviet Communist Party Nomenklatura. As a consequence he was dropped from most of his positions.

Sometime after the Reykjavik meeting in November 1986, Gorbachev promoted Kvitsinsky to be Soviet ambassador to West Germany. He spoke excellent German and for many years had carefully followed the evolution of the political scene there. Nevertheless, he soon became widely distrusted in Germany.

Over the years I came to the conclusion that Kvitsinsky was a deeply unhappy man. He had mastered all the nuances of Soviet political doctrine and could hold forth at length on any aspect of it. He asserted complete support for Stalin, claiming that Stalin had won the Second World War by decreeing that all soldiers attempting to flee the battlefield or to surrender be shot in the back; if he hadn't done so the Soviet Army would have broken up in confusion. Even on that I thought his position to be "tongue in cheek."

In his private conversations with me it appeared that Kvitsinsky was cynical even about the system he claimed to support; I came to suspect that he wished to defect from the Soviet side. He described to me what he had learned about the world trade in diamonds and how it should be possible for the two of us to make a substantial profit on the basis of information he had received from the diamond experts on the Soviet side. I checked the information out with some of my Swiss friends and found that his facts were substantially correct. Walking together in the mountains one day he took me to a Swiss inn for lunch; he had ascertained what it could be bought for and suggested he might do so. I reported all this to my CIA friends in the hope that they might wish to arrange his defection. I do not know whether they tried or not.

Some years later, after the abortive coup by the Soviet hardliners, I learned that, had the coup succeeded, Kvitsinsky would have been made foreign minister. When it failed, he seemed to be in disgrace. But being a survivor he somehow seems to have ended up as one of the staff of the political institute in Moscow that Eduard Shevardnadze had headed prior to the time he decided to become the political leader of Georgia.

The dissatisfaction with different aspects of the Soviet system and its values that Sakharov and Kvitsinsky both expressed in very different ways was widely held throughout the Soviet Union. Most people understood the need for reform. But the nature, degree, and reach of reform and its goals were disputed.

The principal architect of official reform, Mikhail Gorbachev, made his objectives clear. His efforts to overhaul the Communist Party of the Soviet Union and the Soviet system in its last days was not an attempt to recapture the Russian value system: it was an attempt to purify the existing Soviet system and to recapture and reaffirm its values.

I found him to be quite a different type of man than Sakharov. During Gorbachev's early days as general secretary of the Politburo, Roz Ridgway, the Assistant Secretary of State for European Affairs (which included the USSR) and I were part of Secretary George Shultz's team at each of his meetings with the Soviet leadership. I was impressed with Gorbachev's self-confidence, his agility and quickness in the give-and-take of political discussion, and his seeming ability to handle or outmaneuver his Soviet opponents. I believed that, had he been an American, he would have risen to high position even in our quite different society and culture.

It was later, when I studied with care the flow of thought in his book *Perestroika*, which he had gone off to his home one summer to write, that I came to the conclusion that he was serious when he claimed to be a convinced Marxist-Leninist. As he repeatedly reminds us, he is not only a convinced Marxist-Leninist, but a firm believer in the eventual triumph worldwide of socialism in the Soviet sense of the total elimination of capitalism.[1]

It was also apparent from his book that he was ardently anti-Western and, in particular, anti-American.

During our Moscow meeting with him in the fall of 1985,

---

[1] Gorbachev, Mikhail, *Perestroika* (New York: Harper and Row, 1987), pp. 36–38, 44.

Gorbachev told us that in the days when he and Nicolai Ryzhkov were members of the Politburo headed by Yuri Andropov, the two of them talked about the many things that seemed to be wrong with the Soviet Union. The party had become too big, too self-indulgent, and corrupt; it had lost touch with the people. At the same time the economy was in desperate condition with an increasing rate of inflation and a decline in productivity. The armed forces were strong and disciplined but were demanding and receiving a huge percentage of the gross national product. However, the leadership of the Politburo was not politically strong enough to force restraint on the demands of the military. Furthermore, there were growing signs of ethnic rivalries and hatreds.

Gorbachev also told us that during Andropov's regime he and Ryzhkov had assembled a group of a thousand of the brightest and ablest young men to make detailed studies of the Soviet problems and to suggest courses of action to correct them. Thus, according to Gorbachev, when he became General Secretary of the Politburo he and Ryzhkov did not begin his reform efforts from square one: they had a comprehensive array of pertinent studies available. These studies included the concepts of *glasnost* and *perestroika*, a reform of military-civilian relations, and a new approach to ethnic problems.

I doubt that Gorbachev had any comprehension of the driving forces for radical change that *glasnost* and *perestroika* would release in the Russians and other ethnic groups determined to achieve radical, not merely cosmetic, reform. He could persuade himself that turning against corrupt leaders of communist satellites such as Erich Honecker was consistent with his objective of purifying the Communist party so that it would become able and worthy of leading Marxism-Leninism to worldwide ascendancy. The same type of argument justified almost every action that seemed useful for keeping him in power. But it also justified his shying away from taking the decisive actions necessary to deal in time with the Soviet Union's economic and political problems; he could justify delay on the grounds that the timing was wrong; he needed to delay to permit the necessary political support to develop. Gradually his position became more and more untenable.

The upheavals that sprang from Gorbachev's reform efforts eventually destroyed the Soviet system and ended the Soviet Union as a political entity. However, while reformers, or even revolutionaries, could topple the old Soviet administrative and legal structures, refounding a value system to replace the old one was more difficult. Intertwined with the old economic and political system were the remains of decades of assumptions and values cultivated to support them. Much of the prerevolutionary Russian value system that might have replaced the Soviet values had vanished with the Russian culture the Marxist-Leninists tried to eradicate. Without alternative Russian values to many of the imposed Marxist-Leninist ones, the Russian rejection of the Marxist-Leninist system was incomplete.

In the fall of 1992, I was in Moscow as part of an Atlantic Council team to discuss with Russian think-tank and government people what needed to be done to get Russian reform under way and to expedite the country's conversion to democracy and a market economy. Our Russian counterparts described their problem as being twofold. One part concerned specific legislative and administrative actions that were required. The second, and they thought the more important part, was the cultural, political, psychological, and educational task. Conversion to a market economy, they told me, was impossible without a massive educational effort to reform public attitudes.

The Russian population had been inculcated in the belief that individual ownership of property was not only illegal but improper. Some hoped to supplant these ingrained Marxist-Leninist ideas by importing Western economic and political-science literature to help teach new values. However, few books on Western economic thought or jurisprudence were available. It also seemed wiser to try to help the Russians recover a Russian culture more attuned to democracy and market economy instead of encouraging them to adopt an alien American culture. A Russian-value-system foundation would provide a far stronger and more stable basis for the acceptance among the people of a Russian democracy and a Russian market system. But the task is difficult and may take many years.

The experiences of the people of Russia and the Soviet Union confirm the proposition that organic, culturally based value systems are far less brittle or subject to erosion than value systems put together or developed by individuals regardless of how brilliant, persuasive, or ruthless they may be. The Soviet Union and its value system collapsed upon itself. However, the complete restoration of the Russian values needed to heal that nation is complicated by the damage done by the Marxist-Leninists.

It is now 75 years since the October Revolution. The last of the outstanding Russian figures like Sakharov and Shchukin, born around the turn of the century and survivors of the various communist regimes, have died. There now exist only colonies of Russians who have been educated outside of the USSR and are conversant with Russian culture. The Russian authorities responsible for the educational program there are desperate over the lack of people and of printed material necessary to initiate the recovery of their own culture. The Yeltsin government is strapped for money and has understandably placed its highest priority on paying for food and those things necessary for the survival of its population. Funds for education, the payoff from which can only be realized in the future, must be deferred or provided by others such as the West. To assist the Yeltsin government to educate its people appears to be a worthwhile objective of the United States, which could help, to the extent we can afford to do so, the transition of the former Soviet Union toward democracy and a market ecomony.

5

THE PRACTICE
OF POLITICS:
HARRY S TRUMAN
AND AMERICAN HEROES

When Harry S Truman was sworn in as President after the death of Franklin Roosevelt, I was in Europe serving as one of the directors of the U.S. Strategic Bombing Survey. I had never known Truman well, but I had been exposed to him and to people associated with him over a number of years and in a variety of contexts. I was dubious about his qualifications to lead the United States during the closing months of the war in Europe and the longer period that it might take to defeat Japan, but I was more deeply skeptical of his qualifications to guide the United States and the world in general to a constructive peace at the conclusion of the war.

Part of my uneasiness about Truman's qualifications came from his past association with the Pendergast organization in Missouri. I was familiar with Tom Pendergast's political machine from my days as a Wall Street banker at Dillon, Read & Co. when I participated in a battle to wrest control of a utility holding company, United Light and Power, from preacher-turned-promoter Cyrus Eaton. After we managed to gain effective control of the company, I became a director of its principal subsidiary, United Light and Railways Co., which in turn owned

Kansas City Power & Light Co. I found Eaton had made substantial payoffs to Pendergast's people through Kansas City Power & Light Co.

After the failure of his haberdashery, and in desperate need of a job, Truman became a political associate of Pendergast, who helped launch Truman's political career. Pendergast's influence, through his Kansas City political machine, was instrumental in Truman's election to county judge in Jackson County. For me, Truman's past association with this shady organization stirred deep skepticism about his integrity.

I also had some doubts about Truman because of the activities of a member of his wartime committee staff, an investigator named Henry Magee. As a senator, Truman chaired the Senate Special Committee investigating the National Defense Programs, nicknamed the Truman Committee. The committee checked into the propriety of the wartime procurement activities of government agencies. At that time I was part of Henry Wallace's Board of Economic Warfare (BEW), responsible for overseas procurement of strategic materials needed to prosecute the war. One of the most critical shortages was sheet mica, which was needed to make condensers for electronic equipment. The known sources of the material were in India, Brazil, and an inaccessible valley between China and Tibet; no high-quality sheet mica existed in the United States. Promoters in the lower Appalachian mountains pressured Magee to persuade the BEW to buy their domestic mica, which was in rocks containing worthless flecks unusable for military equipment. I had no idea whether Truman had any knowledge of what Magee was up to, but he was part of Truman's organization.

Thus, when I was called back to Washington from my work with the European U.S. Strategic Bombing Survey in 1945, I was deeply worried about our new president. My wife Phyllis had a quite different view. She was working with a nurses' aide group in Washington that Mrs. Truman chaired. She greatly admired Mrs. Truman and insisted that a man who had such a good wife must be a good man. Of course she turned out to be right and my skepticism unjustified.

A few days after I returned to Washington, President Truman asked some of us who had conducted the survey of the effectiveness of strategic air power in the European theater to conduct a somewhat similar survey in the Pacific theater. However, he widened the scope of our task; we were to cover the role and effectiveness of air power as a whole, not just strategic air power. Moreover, we were to analyze and report on the effects of the atomic weapons dropped at Hiroshima and Nagasaki, find out why the Japanese attacked us at Pearl Harbor, and why they sued for peace when they did. Lastly, we were to give him our recommendations as to how the U.S. defense establishment should be organized in the future to best take account of the lessons learned during World War II.

Most of the others who had worked on the survey in Europe wanted to get back to their peacetime jobs, so I was left in effective control of the Pacific Survey. We rapidly assembled a competent team of several thousand members including 500 scientists and other experts specifically assigned to analyze and report on the effects of the Hiroshima and Nagasaki atomic weapons. My principal difficulty was in working out an acceptable working relationship between my team and General Douglas MacArthur, who had no respect for President Truman or for civilian authority in general.

President Truman handled MacArthur with extraordinary patience. He respected the leadership MacArthur had demonstrated during the Pacific War, the hero worship many Americans gave him, and the enormous support he enjoyed in the Congress. He had shown similar patience with General Dwight Eisenhower in 1947 when Eisenhower was Chief of the General Staff of the Army and insisted, contrary to Truman's judgment, that all our remaining troops be removed from South Korea.

Truman's caution and hesitation in handling Eisenhower and MacArthur contrasts strongly with the courage and decisiveness he showed in February 1947 when the British informed him they could no longer support Greece and Turkey against the enormous pressure of the Soviet Union and guerrillas it supported. The British found themselves too exhausted after two world wars to continue their heroic, and at times lonely, defense of Western values. With little hesitation President Truman picked up the challenge. He made a twofold decision: the United States should take the lead in creating a working political and economic order in the noncommunist world, and that the United States should participate actively in defending that world against attacks mounted by people with antithetical aspirations for the future led by the communist leaders in Moscow.

Mr. Truman's February 1947 decision was followed by an extraordinary series of actions embodied in the policy of containing Soviet expansionism. These included the Truman Doctrine and the Greek-Turkish Aid Program, the Marshall Plan, the North Atlantic Alliance, and accepting the challenge of the surprise attack by the North Koreans backed by Moscow and Peking upon South Korea. This was the beginning of the forty-year attempt by one Soviet regime after another to halt the efforts of the United States to create and defend an international system favorable to liberal political and economic values.

Early in his presidency, Truman made similarly forceful and difficult decisions on certain domestic issues. When the railroad unions threatened what would have amounted to a general strike, he signed an executive order nationalizing the railroads in such an event, subjecting any labor union leaders who violated the order to injunction and contempt of court charges. The railroad workers went back to work. Later, he ran into even greater recalcitrance from John L. Lewis, the czar of the United Mine Workers. Again, the President stood rock firm and John L. Lewis had to back down.

Truman also showed determination in carrying out his wish that the United States be the first to recognize the creation of Israel, despite the almost equally determined resistance of General George C. Marshall, then Secretary of State. Marshall was backed by almost everyone in the State Department, including Robert Lovett, Loy Henderson, Chip Bohlen, Dean Acheson, Dean Rusk, George Kennan and I, as well as many outside the State Department, including Jim Forrestal. Many of us thought Truman was motivated by domestic political considerations, but probably he also had early made up his mind as a result of the Holocaust that the Jews were entitled to a homeland of their own.

The fact that Truman had courage and conviction does not mean that his decisions were always wise or his judgment of people reliable. I had little sympathy with his adamancy in holding the defense budget down to $13 billion at a time of growing Soviet strength and aggressiveness. The constricted budget weakened our military services, particularly the Army. His appointment in 1949 of Louis Johnson, who had no qualifications for the job, to be Secretary of Defense, was an irresponsible decision that Truman himself came to regret.

Why was Truman so decisive in certain contexts but so timid

and dilatory in others? I believe that, by nature, Truman was determined and decisive, but as president he quickly recognized the political difficulties of pursuing a bold foreign policy without the consensus of the people and a sufficiently receptive Congress to make effective leadership possible. The constitutional division of powers, particularly between the legislative and executive branches of government, is of supreme importance in American politics. The key to effective leadership for any president is his ability to work with Congress, a requirement that often results in great presidential caution in the face of potential opposition to his policy.

Truman's problems with General MacArthur were an example of the potential political difficulties of policy. There were some in the administration with reservations about appointing General MacArthur the commander of the UN forces in Korea while reporting to a United Nations multinational committee. The moment C. B. "Burt" Marshall, who joined the Policy Planning Staff in 1950, heard of the proposed command arrangements, he came to me in protest. Burt knew well certain of his former associates who had worked with MacArthur. It was their view, shared by Burt, that only an unambiguous chain of authority above him could keep MacArthur in line; a multinational committee would not do. We on the Policy Planning Staff quickly agreed with Burt.

In the hope of averting trouble, we immediately talked to John D. Hickerson, then Assistant Secretary of State for United Nations Affairs. He told us we were too late; he had already lined up the British, the French, and others. Had we been able to implement Burt's advice in time, President Truman's problems with MacArthur, and the near destruction of American forces in their advance to the Yalu could have been avoided.

When it became evident that he had to relieve General MacArthur to preserve the authority of the presidency, Truman did so reluctantly in April 1951 and then only after having delayed longer than I thought he should have. Of course, he was right, both in deciding that General MacArthur had to be relieved and in realizing that to do so would have serious domestic political repercussions. In fact, doing so denied him any possibility of reelection in 1952.

I came to greatly admire Mr. Truman as a paradigm for me and many of my generation. He had the virtues of the midwestern common man. He was not a college man and he suffered all the hardships of economic depression, including the failure of his haberdashery. He fulfilled the American dream that an average citizen can be president and succeed in being a good president.

The characteristic that in my judgment made him a great president was derived from the interest in history that he had absorbed from his high school history teacher, Margaret Phelps. She induced him to study Greek and Roman history; from this he acquired a respect for the responsibilities of high office. In particular, he had a keen sense of duty to uphold the role and dignity of the office of the American presidency. He resolved to maintain the high standards expected of a holder of that office.

In carrying out that intention, Truman gathered about himself the very best men he could find to advise him on the crucial decisions he, as president, would have to make concerning the nation's security. Initially, General George C. Marshall served as his Secretary of State, to be replaced in 1949 by Dean Acheson. In the fall of 1950 Truman was able to replace Louis Johnson as Secretary of Defense with General Marshall. Thereafter, he had the two men he wanted to rely upon in the two positions crucial to national security.

Acheson and Marshall were the two wisest and most experienced men of their generation, and Truman earned and held the complete loyalty of both. Neither of them ever had the slightest doubt as to who was President, neither did either hesitate to tell the President what they thought, not merely what they thought he might wish to hear. There was, however, one instance in which Acheson had serious reservations about doing so.

Going into his office to see Acheson one day, I recommended he propose to the President the firing of General Harry Vaughan, a personal assistant, and William O'Dwyer, at the time U.S. Ambassador to Mexico. Vaughan was improperly using his friendship with Truman, which stemmed from World War I when each commanded an artillery battery. O'Dwyer was a political crony of doubtful reputation.

Acheson protested that if he did as I had recommended, Truman would just throw him out of his office. I then asked Acheson a few questions. Did he agree that Truman would eventually have to fire General MacArthur? Acheson concurred. I then asked whether he agreed that when the President did so, it would explode into a major domestic political crisis? He agreed with that too.

"Do you agree that Mr. Truman will be in a better position to weather the criticism he's bound to encounter if he first puts his own house in order?" I then asked.

Dean replied that he did.

Finally, I asked, "Then aren't you duty-bound to recommend to the President what you believe to be the wise course, even if you doubt it is a recommendation he is likely to accept?"

"Damn you!" he exclaimed, and threw up his hands.

Dean did what I had suggested. He went over to Blair House, where Mr. Truman was living while the White House was being renovated, and advised him that Vaughan and O'Dwyer should be relieved of their official duties. Just as Dean had predicted, Truman was adamant and flatly refused. Eventually, of course, he did have to fire MacArthur and that action did cause a serious domestic crisis.

On those issues he considered of no concern to the "Office of the Presidency," Truman felt free to follow his own, more human instinct. When Paul Hume, the *Washington Post*'s music critic, commented adversely on Margaret Truman's voice in a concert at Constitution Hall, Mr. Truman composed a handwritten letter to Hume, put a stamp on it, and had a White House messenger, Samuel Mitchell, drop it in a public mailbox.

The letter was hardly in "presidential" style. Among other things, it said: "Someday I hope to meet you. When that happens you'll need a new nose, a lot of beefsteak for black eyes, and perhaps a supporter below. [Westbook] Pegler, a gutter snipe, is a gentleman alongside of you. I hope you'll accept that statement as a worse insult than a reflection on your ancestry."[1]

During his presidency a majority of Americans admired Truman. What they admired most was his feisty style in attacking the Republican-controlled Congress and in his subsequent surprise victory over Tom Dewey in the 1948 election. Essentially, there was an underlying feeling that he understood the grassroots character of the country and was supporting it courageously and wisely. He didn't flinch when things went against him. For my generation he was an example of an American hero for this century.

But what does a "hero" such as Truman represent in contem-

[1]   McCullough, David, *Truman* (New York: Simon & Schuster, 1992), pp. 828-829.

porary America? There are changing sources and measures of heroes and heroism in a nation now taught to embrace the empirical over the mythical and to be skeptical of values. In classical literature and myth, whether Greek, Roman, Nordic, Muslim, or Oriental, heroes emerged in a context of hundreds or even thousands of years of experience. Stories about heroes were often handed down in oral tradition from generation to generation. These heroes grew to personify aspirations and ideals of men standing strong against nature, and in human triumph and disaster. They filled specific roles and psychic needs in their culture, whether they were real or fictional people. Heroes expressed the souls and value systems of local tribes bound to specific areas of land and water in times quire different from our rootless world of global interaction.

Today, "hero" seems to have acquired a different, vaguer, almost superficial meaning of admiration. I have asked some of my grandchildren and their friends, whose ages range between twelve and fifteen, whom they consider their heroes. My grandsons all named sports figures. Some of their friends mentioned Franklin Roosevelt and Abraham Lincoln; none mentioned Harry Truman. It may well be that only a few members of my generation share my view of Truman as a heroic character.

Perhaps the role of heroes and heroism is greater in other contemporary cultures than in America. In India, respect for Gandhi dominated a century. In Iran, Khomeini inspired fanatical loyalty in millions of fundamentalist adherents, and a willingness to sacrifice their lives for his cause. Between the world wars, Adolf Hitler and Benito Mussolini aspired to be, and occasionally became, heroes to their followers. In the Soviet Union, the cult of personality caused the entire Soviet communist system to revolve about a series of totalitarian dictators. In these later cases, the corrupting influences of power, suspect values, and the abuses of false heroes quickly became evident, and their supporting ideologies, often created to advance the "heroes" themselves, collapsed in war and revolution.

Many nations and cultures place more emphasis upon closer, more binding communal relations and a stronger sense of common values and unity than upon heroes and charismatic leadership. Most such nations have relatively small populations, from three to twenty million. Political circumstances have permitted them to escape foreign domination, or perhaps they have existed at the edges of the old Cold War coalitions as disinterested neutrals. Some of them may have a unique language, difficult for others to learn and understand. Some examples would be Finland, Hungary, Israel, and perhaps Austria, although Viennese German is not much different than that spoken in Berlin, Hanover, or Frankfurt.

Often the bonds of race, nationality, common history, and common loyalties are stronger if a culture perceives itself as a small but unified group in the alien sea of world civilization (using the term as Spengler would). Sometimes adversity itself may forge stronger bonds of cultural, religion, or community, an event repeated in history. Israel, despite its internal tensions, fits this description.

Looking back through history, one finds tremendous variety among the strong and persisting cultures and the resolve of their people in adversity. I was once struck by the thesis advanced in *The Mind of Latin Christendom*, by Edward Motley Pickman. Pickman addresses how the core of Greco-Roman wisdom and tradition survived after the fall of Rome through the Dark Ages, during which the population of Rome dwindled from some million or more to a few thousand virtual savages.

Pickman argues that Greco-Roman culture was preserved through the efforts of the old Roman senatorial families who had large landed estates in the Italian countryside. After converting to Christianity during the days of Constantine, it was they who protected Christian monasteries from the depredations of ravening barbarians. These monasteries carefully preserved manuscripts containing the works of Aristotle, Plato, the Christian fathers, and the essence of Roman culture. Without the guardianship of Roman aristocratic and Christian values, which recognized the importance of protecting this wisdom and tradition, Greco-Roman culture may not have survived to its renaissance.[2]

The preservation of values in the face of adversity and in the struggle between the empirical and mythical, as well as the role of heroism in that struggle, remains a challenge for individuals and nations. In the early postwar years, a friend of mine, Lewis Gallantiere, introduced me to the work of Lesek Kolakowski, a former ideologist in the Polish Communist Party. Kolakowski had become convinced of the essential evil of the Communist Party as it evolved pursuing the precepts of Lenin and Stalin, and wrote passionately against it. He was expelled from Poland in 1968 and went first to England and later to the University of Chicago where he is now a Senior Fellow with the John M. Olin Center for Inquiry into the Theory and Practice of Democracy.

Kolakowski's major work is his three-volume *Main Currents of Marxism*, which many, including myself, consider the authoritative work on the subject. However, while still in Poland in 1966, he wrote a profound and difficult work, *The Presence of Myth*,

---

[2]   Pickman, Edward M., *The Mind of Latin Christendom* (New York: Oxford University Press, 1937), p. 132.

published first in French and only recently translated into English. It was written at a time when many western logicians had reached a dead end, and those such as Alfred N. Whitehead, Bertrand Russell, and Kurt Gödel had demonstrated the limits of self-consistent systems of rational thought and the need to search outside such systems to answer a wide range of fundamental questions. In particular, questions of values beyond confounding empirical answers often required insights of revelation.

In studying similar questions, Kolakowski observes that myths, as they have evolved over millennia, have some claim to probable truth in dealing with the fundamental issues of all societies, "the questions of origin, of truth, of beauty, of heroism, of relation to nature, to the animal kingdom, to space and to eternity." He asks, why not give the insights derived from myth and its heroes the benefit of the doubt against purely rational systems whose limitations and inadequacies can be demonstrated by the inadequacies of their own internal logic?[3]

Kolakowski notes that two value systems, empirical and mythical, are present in each of us. This paradoxical coexistence is both inevitable and seemingly impossible; the tension between the two produces the fine essence of civilization. Our culture thrives on the tension between the desire to achieve the synthesis of the conflicting systems and its inability to do so. To achieve the synthesis, or to abandon the effort, would be the death of culture.[4] Scientists have dealt with analogous opposites through the doctrine of complementarity. Mao Tse-tung dealt with them through his doctrine of the unity through contradiction.

To some, such as Allan Bloom, the tension between value sys-

[3]   Kolakowski, Leszek, *The Presence of Myth* (University of Chicago Press, 1989).

[4]   *Ibid.*, p. 135.

tems in contemporary America has gone from the search for a synthesis and truth into a battle over the preservation of ideas and values themselves as expressed in philosophy. Bloom sees such a struggle within American universities that he feels have abandoned their search for truth. He put forth his views in his well-known book, *The Closing of the American Mind*, which was a runaway publishing success. I believe its popularity sprang from its vigorous polemic on the undoubted decline in the literacy, knowledge, and reasoning skills of the American public.

Bloom blames the decay of contemporary learning and education upon the value relativism of university elites. To him, higher education has embraced the belief that truth is relative, and therefore the Socratic examined life, and the pursuit of philosophy aimed at discovering truth with its implied values, is impossible. If truth is relative, so are its attendant values and the value systems they engender. Without a belief in truth, reasons Bloom, universities no longer try to teach a unified concept of interrelated knowledge, one which tries to offer a holistic view of the world and of values. Instead, education and learning occur out of context and without purpose, and universities fall victim to popular political opinion. At American universities, he argues, "[w]estern rationalism has culminated in a rejection of reason."[5]

To restore balance, Bloom calls for a return to a pure university, one in which learning and education help students and scholars seek truth and are not simply used to justify prevailing popular sentiments. Just as political responsibility for freedom falls upon our government, the fate of philosophy, which preserves the values of that freedom, falls upon American universities.

---

[5]   Bloom, Allan, *The Closing of the American Mind* (New York: Simon & Schuster, 1987), p. 240.

While many of Bloom's observations were on the mark, and his criticisms justified, I was less sure of the causes for the decline than he. I was also skeptical of the sort of university he seemed to imply: devoted to abstract philosophical discussion and devoid of interest in positive action. I felt that the university elite Bloom advocated would isolate itself from political life, separating theorists from practitioners.

I wrote Bloom a critical letter questioning the title of his book, which I thought should have been *Toward the Recovery of the American University*, and arguing that something more than an exemplary was needed: someone had to play the Plato to Socrates, the St. Peter to Jesus. We needed thoughtful leadership. In answer, Bloom agreed that the title of his book was his publisher's doing and probably inappropriate to the subject matter, but he did not respond to my criticism of his recommendations. He did ask me to attend a postgraduate seminar he conducted on heroes and heroism, and to present a paper on Truman as a hero of my generation. The paper contained much the same thoughts as I here describe. However, I do not believe he was interested in the broader implications of what he advocated. At least he and his associates did not seem interested in the subject they asked me to discuss.

A modern American hero should be more than the paradigm of the ideals of his time, he should both think and act. He should inspire Americans with a forward-looking set of values. All the great presidents, including George Washington, Thomas Jefferson, Abraham Lincoln, both Roosevelts, Woodrow Wilson, Harry Truman, and Ronald Reagan, were able to do so. Truman transmitted the sense of the leader's responsibility to the office he held into an American political philosophy appropriate to his time.

6

FURTHER ON THE PRACTICE OF POLITICS: JAMES FORRESTAL AND THE WILL TO SUCCEED

The spring of 1929 was close to the peak of the long industrial boom that preceded the stock market crash of October 1929 and the Great Depression of the early 1930s. I was less than a year out of college, I had been ill the preceding fall and I was unable to go on to graduate work. Instead, I worked in Bridgeport, Connecticut as an accountant for a small factory of the Container Corporation of America, where I rose to the position of office manager.

After six months, I had learned as much about accounting as I wished to learn, so I resigned from my job and worked out an arrangement to go to Germany for Bacon-Whipple & Co., a Chicago firm of investment bankers. In Germany I was to prepare a report on whether it made sense for their clients to buy German securities rather than pay the high prices in relation to earnings of American securities. At the suggestion of Edith Ames, the mother of one of my classmates at Harvard, I called on Clarence Dillon, senior partner of one of the leading investment banking firms in New York, Dillon, Read & Co., to ask him for letters of introduction to friends of his in Germany who might help me understand the German economic, financial, and political scene so I could do the analytical work necessary for my report.

Dillon was highly skeptical of my qualifications to do such an analysis and even more skeptical of whether anyone would pay any attention to my recommendations in the unlikely case that they turned out to have merit: I was barely twenty-two years old. But he was sufficiently interested to invite me to lunch in his private dining room on the fortieth floor of the Equitable Building which was across the street from Dillon, Read & Co.'s offices.

While we were having lunch, James Forrestal, a partner in his firm, walked in unannounced and began to talk to Mr. Dillon. "The men on the corner (meaning J. P. Morgan & Co.) have just arranged a merger of the National Park Bank into the Guaranty Trust Company," he said. "That will give them control over the largest commercial bank in New York. I recommend we counter that move by merging the National Bank of Commerce into the Chase Bank. That will balance Morgan's influence in the commercial banking world with Dillon Read's."

Dillon said he agreed and then asked how Forrestal proposed to proceed. Forrestal replied that he had arranged to see Charles McCain, the President of the Chase Bank, at three the next afternoon. Dillon interjected that he thought it better not to wait until afternoon, but to see McCain in the morning. Forrestal objected, saying he was busy in the morning but would see McCain at three in the afternoon.

This introduction to Forrestal left a deep impression upon me. I saw him as a man who understood the world of Wall Street and its power politics, was quick to understand what needed to be done next, and was prepared to do it. This was my first exposure to a man of action: in terms of this book, a man fully engaged in the "practice" rather than the theory of politics.

In September of 1929, I returned to New York after completing my report about Germany. In it, I concluded that Germany's economic situation had been weakened by the burden of reparations payments, that its financial situation was precarious because of the large outstanding volume of German short-term borrowing abroad that might not be renewed in the event of an economic downturn, and that the political situation within the country was too fragile to withstand the pressures of even a mild economic contraction. I concluded that anyone who invested in Germany at that time should have his head examined. Clarence Dillon considered my analysis persuasive although its conclusions were at odds with that of his advisors. He asked me to join the staff of Dillon, Read & Co. and on October 1, 1929 I became his personal assistant.

During those initial days I saw little of Forrestal or the other partners; I was working on projects Dillon directly assigned to me, or on other projects of my own initiative. I was viewed with suspicion by the partners. It was only after an important transaction that I had fostered on my own had gone sour and I had descended into the doghouse of Dillon's disapproval that Forrestal and the other partners decided I might be helpful to them. Most of them, at one time or another, had also fallen athwart Dillon's displeasure.

After some years of working with Forrestal at Dillon, Read, I got to know quite well both him and his wife Jo, a former editor of *Vogue*. They lived in a handsome house on Beekman Place overlooking the East River, and from time to time I would go up there to deliver papers for Jim to read or sign. It was obvious that the marriage was an unhappy one, but Jim was a Catholic and divorce was not possible. Jo drank too much and took long trips to Europe. Jim separated himself from his home life as much as he could and seemed to show little interest in his wife or children.

Eventually, I managed to break through some of Forrestal's shell of privacy and reticence, discovering more of his warmer side. One day, I had something important to consult him about and walked into his office without knocking. He was on the telephone with someone in Beacon, New York, arranging a major personal contribution to a boys' club there. Forrestal was annoyed at my intrusion, probably because he wanted to protect the tough unbending image that he thought enhanced his effectiveness. He looked the part, with the face of a tough Irish boxer—he had, in fact, broken his nose in a boxing match.

Later, when we became closer friends, Jim told me about his youth in Matteawan, New York. He described his father as an attractive Irishman who liked to drink more than was good for him and his mother as a firm Catholic matriarch who had wished him to become a priest. Financed by his father, he went first to Dartmouth, but after a year transferred to Princeton University where he never completed his requirements for a degree. At that time, it appears that he went through an emotional break with his mother and with Catholicism.

Forrestal once told me that the guiding influence on his life had not been his parents or his education but the homely wisdom of the town blacksmith in Matteawan, the town neighboring Beacon where he was born. He used to hang around the smithy after school, where the blacksmith took an interest in him and gave him a new outlook on life. It was the blacksmith's view that "will" was everything. If Jim were truly determined to succeed in what he chose to do, the blacksmith had no doubt that he could succeed. Jim wanted to be respected by his classmates at school, he wanted to go to college, he wanted to be active in business, he wanted to make a lot of money, he wanted to be a success. He later attributed his iron will and his determination to succeed to the strong influence of the Matteawan blacksmith.

Jim originally seemed to have little understanding of foreign affairs. His later interest stemmed in part from a business need, his association with Captain "Cap" Reber, the principal executive officer of the Texas Oil Company, a client of Dillon, Read. Texas Oil had a worldwide petroleum products distribution system, including an important subsidiary in Nazi Germany, from which the company withdrew when Hitler began his aggression. Jim's close involvement with Texas Oil came after the outbreak of war in Europe threatened the survival of the company's distribution system. American crude oil and oil products had become too expensive to compete in world markets and Texas Oil needed access to foreign sources of crude oil. Reber had invested heavily in the Barco concession in Colombia, but the enterprise failed.

At about the same time, Standard Oil of California had obtained a concession in Saudi Arabia and hired Everett DeGolyer to study the geology of the country to estimate its future reserves. DeGolyer had long been a close associate of Dillon, Read. He was the first to have a clear view of the probable extent of Persian Gulf oil reserves, particularly those in Saudi Arabia.

Jim concluded that a joint venture between Standard Oil of California and Texas Oil could be of immense value to both. Standard had no worldwide distribution to market its Saudi Arabian oil products; Texas Oil had a distribution system but no foreign oil production. Jim flew to California to convince the executives of Standard of the merits of the idea. The result became Caltex, which controlled both Aramco, Standard's subsidiary in Saudi Arabia, and Texas Oil's worldwide distribution system. Over the years it has been one of the world's most successful and profitable enterprises.

About this time, Jim also developed an interest in political theory and became knowledgeable in communism and other basic political ideologies. His interest was tied to my own investigations into the political and social upheavals in Europe and the Soviet Union.

By the summer of 1937, I had become deeply concerned about the hold and influence of fascism in Italy, Nazism in Germany, and communism in the Soviet Union, as well as the future of those nations under increasingly totalitarian regimes. I had learned as much as I could from reading the literature available on political doctrine, including Spengler's *Decline of the West*. However, I was dissatisfied by the answers I found there. Something was deeply wrong in Spengler's forecasts and prescriptions for action, but I was not certain where the fallacy lay in his basic ideas. I decided to resign from Dillon, Read and return to Harvard for a year or perhaps more of graduate study to find answers to my questions.

At Harvard I learned much about the philosophy, sociology, and background of fascism, Nazism, and communism. One of my professors, George Pettee, had written what I thought was a brilliant book, *The Process of Revolution*, and I gave a copy to Jim Forrestal who read it with great interest. He eventually hired Ed Willett, a former staff assistant to Ferdinand Eberstadt, and directed him to study and teach him the theory behind dialectical materialism. This tutoring became Jim's first intense investigation into political movements around the world.

In May 1940, after I had returned to Dillon, Read, Jim asked me to come to his office. He said that he had received a visit from Paul Shields, head of a leading Wall Street brokerage firm and a friend of his. They were both Democrats, in those days a rare occurrence on Wall Street. Paul had just returned from Washington where he had met with President Roosevelt. In the past, Roosevelt told him, the foundation of his politics had been his attacks on Wall Street and, borrowing Theodore Roosevelt's words, "other malefactors of great wealth." Now, however, he saw Hitler as the greater threat to American and world interests and he wished to build bridges with Wall Street in order to present a unified front. He needed help in doing so.

The President asked Shields to recommend a Democrat respected by the Wall Street community who would be willing to move to Washington to serve as a member of his "silent six," special assistants recently authorized by Congress to work with him during those difficult days. Shields recommended Forrestal for the post. Jim wanted my advice as to whether he should accept.

I asked Jim whether he thought he would be effective in such a job. Jim said he didn't know; he had never worked in Washington and had no experience with how one got things done there. I asked him what he would do if it turned out he could not be effective there. He said he probably would return to Dillon, Read. I then asked him if he turned down the job, would he later have regrets that he had not given himself the opportunity to work with issues of broader scope than those of Wall Street. He said, yes, he thought he would.

"Under those circumstances you have answered your own question," I told him. "If the job does not turn out well, you can return to Dillon, Read & Co. with little loss. If you don't go, you will be plagued with recurring regrets that you didn't give yourself a chance to see what you can do in the broader framework

of national and international affairs. It might work out well."
Jim went.

A few weeks later, I was down in Louisiana completing a financing deal for the United Gas Company (now the Pennzoil Corporation) when I received a cryptic telegram. "Be in Washington Monday morning. Forrestal." The next day I was there. Thus began the fifty subsequent years of my life in Washington with most of my work intimately involved with the U.S. government, its policies, and actions—the day-to-day practice of politics.

By the time I joined him, Jim had developed close relations with those near the President, including Harry Hopkins, Tom Corcoran, Ben Cohen, Jim Rowe, and the principal people in the State Department, the Treasury, the War Department, and the Navy. Simultaneously, he had cultivated the Washington press corps, the most important figure being Arthur Krock, a former classmate at Princeton and head of the Washington Bureau of *The New York Times*.

Jim was already deeply involved in the tasks assigned him by the president. No one was certain where Hitler would make his next move after the fall of France. A quick thrust south through Spain and down the west coast of Africa to the point closest to South America, together with German and Italian subversion in South America, represented a potential threat to the southern half of the Western Hemisphere. Jim and I worked out a secret arrangement with Juan Trippe and Henry Friendly, the president and general counsel respectively of Pan American World Airways, under which Pan Am constructed six airfields in the Caribbean, which could, if necessary, be converted to military use. This would give the U.S. air control of the Caribbean not only for strategic reasons but as a counter to German submarines in the Gulf of Mexico.

An even greater problem was the coordination of U.S. cultural and commercial policies toward Latin America. Despite the "Good Neighbor" policy initiated in the thirties, our relations with the governments and peoples of Latin America were in disarray. Accusations of Yankee imperialism continued to hover over our efforts. In addition, the many immigrants from Germany and Italy who had arrived in Latin America during the 1930s had set up what often had become flourishing businesses. These sometimes dominated local economies. As a result, many Latin Americans felt more bound to the Axis powers than to their neighbor to the north. Such close relations between the Axis and Latin America, of course, would represent a serious threat to our southern flank if Germany and Italy could succeed in subverting the Latin American republics through economic and psychological pressures.

Jim believed that the State Department, as then constituted, was manned by those trained only to observe and report on what was going on at the diplomatic level in Latin America. These diplomats had no training or experience, or natural instinct, to act and mobilize action by others to foster U.S. interests in Latin America, particularly in economic, cultural, and public-opinion matters. He considered the department too large an organization to be quickly retrained or remanned by people with those skills. Jim concluded that a new organization was needed, reporting directly to the president, composed of those having the necessary skills to draw on and coordinate the actions of the line department agencies to get the job done. He asked me to draft a directive creating such an organization. With help from others on the White House staff, particularly from Jim Rowe, another of the six special assistants to the President authorized by act of Congress, we did so.

Forrestal approved the directive, but when I suggested he take it to President Roosevelt to get it signed, he demurred; the time, he said, was not yet ripe. He had discussed the idea at length with top people in the State, Agriculture, Commerce, and Treasury departments. Each had reservations even though they had no alternative solutions. Forrestal decided that if the President signed the directive at that time, the departments would consider that solution to have been imposed on them. If he bided his time, they would themselves come to the conclusion that there was no good alternative course and would ask him to take the directive to the President for approval. Then they would be likely to support the new organization rather than fight it. Jim, of course, was right. My impatience to move forward before the situation was politically ripe would have been counterproductive.

As we were finishing our work creating the Office of the Co-ordinator of Inter-American Affairs, President Roosevelt announced Jim's appointment as Undersecretary to Frank Knox, Secretary of the Navy. Jim was sensitive to the Navy view that outsiders needed to demonstrate their singleminded dedication to the Navy before the Navy could have confidence in them. So, he explained to me, he did not wish me to accompany him. Within a few weeks he was fully accepted by the uniformed Navy; the fact that he had been trained as a Navy pilot during World War I helped. Seeing to it that procurement of ships, guns, ammunition, and other materiel was done wisely, efficiently, and in full conformity with law and legislative intent was the heart of the Undersecretary's job.

Jim recruited an outstanding team of lawyers to help him in that task including Struve Hensel from Milbank Tweed in New York and John Kenney, a distinguished lawyer from Los Angeles. But the uniformed Navy had to perform a central part of the job.

Rear Admiral Samuel M. Robinson was assigned to head that part of the work. Jim asked me to help the admiral bridge the civilian and naval tasks, but by that time I was working on other matters. I recommended H. B. (Ted) Baldwin, a younger former partner in Dillon, Read & Co. Ted joined Robinson's staff and did the job well. During the next four years I continued to keep in reasonably close touch with Jim and considered myself to be one of his close personal friends.

At times, Jim found the pressure of his work and the appearance of being "the tough man of will" hard to maintain. My sister Pussy and her husband Walter Paepcke once found him hiding among the palm trees and bushes surrounding the Palm Court in the lobby of the Plaza Hotel in New York. He emerged from his hiding place and joined them for tea and then dinner. He explained that from time to time he liked to watch people going about their normal business or just enjoying themselves. For relaxation, Jim played golf or tennis at his favorite club, the Chevy Chase Club. It was a pleasure to be with him when he was relaxed.

During the early months of his service with the Navy, Jim confronted one naval disaster after another in the Pacific. I was in South America during the weeks immediately before and after Pearl Harbor, but during the subsequent trials of the Navy and Marine Corps at the Coral Sea, Guadalcanal, and the channel going north toward Bougainville and Rabaul, I frequently saw Jim and other top Navy people. Those were most difficult days. Many mistakes were made and were taken advantage of by the able and professional Japanese Navy.

Jim was pretty well excluded from the operational decisions of the Navy. Admiral Ernest J. King, Chief of Naval Operations, had little use for civilian control. He insisted that the Navy's operational decision-making process go up and down the chain of officers between himself and the various fleets.

In 1944, I left the Foreign Economic Administration where for four years I had been responsible for overseas procurement of strategic materials. I became a director of the U.S. Strategic Bombing Survey (USSBS) and my new work intersected more directly with Jim's. I saw him more often.

There were three spheres where our interests touched. One was future military operations against Japan aimed at forcing the Japanese to surrender. We in the USSBS (pronounced uzz-buzz) had come to the conclusion that a submarine and mining campaign designed to cut off all Japanese movement by sea with the mainland and among the main Japanese islands, reinforced by an air campaign to segment rail and road movement within each island, and direct bombardment attacks on Japanese military installations could bring about a Japanese surrender by November 1945. We thought that a ground invasion of Honshu aimed at capturing the emperor, diplomatic efforts to get the Russians to come into the war, or the use of atomic weapons on Japanese targets were all undesirable and unnecessary.

Jim was in general agreement with our analysis but had a serious reservation about certain implications of our proposal for action. He pointed out that the U.S. had some ten million men under arms in the Pacific. It was politically difficult to leave those men out there with little or nothing to do, but we could not prudently send large numbers of them home until the Japanese had actually surrendered. The timetable we in USSBS had proposed might work out, but no one could have absolute confidence in it.

I suggested that if those men could not be brought home, then we might give them a temporary task that would help mold the strategic future in the Far East along lines favorable to U.S. interests. I asked whether it would be possible for our forces to land on the Chinese mainland and drive a corridor up toward Manchuria, thus dividing Japanese forces in Central China from those in Manchuria. He suggested I take the idea up with Fred Searles, who was both an USSBS director and a deputy to James Byrnes in his capacity as Director of War Mobilization, who reported directly to the President. I did so.

Byrnes discussed the idea with President Roosevelt, who consulted Admiral William D. Leahy, his military advisor. Leahy recommended that the President consult with the Chiefs of Staff on the proposal. They turned down idea and insisted that we plan to invade the Island of Honshu and capture the Emperor, which they saw as the sole sure road to victory. The decision to use the atomic weapons at Hiroshima and Nagasaki flowed from that decision. Their use seemed preferable to the millions of casualties, including 500,000 American dead or seriously wounded, that would probably accompany an invasion directed at capturing the Emperor.

Another sphere in which our responsibilities crossed concerned the recommendations of USSBS on the postwar organization of the U.S. defense establishment and the roles and missions of the three services to be created within a unified Department of Defense. In the draft of our report on postwar defense structure we recommended that the Navy be given the mission of achieving, in the event of war, control of the surface of the seas, the air above the seas, and the waters below, and then of exploiting that control for whatever purposes higher authority were to direct. The Army was to have the mission of achieving control over pertinent land areas and of exploiting that control; it was also to have command over the air forces assigned the task of close air support of those ground forces. A third service was to have command over those forces assigned the mission of destroying targets deep in the territory of the enemy that would paralyze the opponent's capability and will to sustain his war effort. It was also to have the mission of defending targets in the U.S. that the enemy might wish to destroy. In addition, the third force should have the task, in conjunction with the efforts of the air components of the other two services, of achieving overall command of the air. Each of the three services would be entitled to have whatever types of equipment it thought most effective in carrying out its tasks and that it could afford to acquire.

I discussed this concept with Admiral Forrest Sherman, Chief of Naval Operations, who was sympathetic, and with Jim, who also agreed. But at the subsequent Key West conference on service roles and missions the concept was rejected. Instead, the conference adopted a system allocating the roles and missions of the services on the basis of the types of weapon systems each service was permitted to acquire. Interservice hostility and rivalry stemming from the Key West decision was to be a major factor in the subsequent unification debates and in Forrestal's difficulties with the services when he became the first Secretary of Defense in 1947.

A third sphere of interaction between Jim and me concerned U.S. policy toward the Middle East and the creation in Palestine of an independent Israeli state. The Truman Doctrine, promulgated in March 1947, settled the issue of United States presence in the Middle East. But it did not settle the issue of whether our primary interest revolved about relations with the Arab states on the one hand (which included, in Forrestal's mind, the growing future influence of those states due to their vast oil reserves); or on our sympathy with the Jews who had survived the Holocaust and wished a homeland of their own in Palestine.

Forrestal strongly favored the first alternative. As I mentioned before, there were a number of others in U.S. policy circles who shared that view, including General Marshall, Robert Lovett, Loy Henderson in charge of Middle Eastern affairs at the State Department, Chip Bohlen, me, and a large number of others. But Forrestal was the most persistent and forceful. He was later bitterly attacked by those fostering the Zionist point of view. Urged on by David K. Niles, Truman's administrative assistant acting as his liaison with the Jewish community, and backed by his special counsel Clark Clifford, the president insisted that the U.S. be the first to recognize Israel and thereafter did not deviate in his support for it.

Later, I shared Jim's worry that unlimited Jewish immigration into Palestine would make U.S. problems increasingly unmanageable with the Arabs. It was my view that it would be helpful if we could find an alternate location for a second Jewish home. During the war, the Foreign Economic Administration had financed the mining and refinement of bauxite in Surinam (formerly Dutch Guiana). As a result, I knew the area. The highlands above the escarpment in Surinam offered an almost wholly uninhabited but naturally rich area suitable for creating such a homeland. I talked to representatives of the Dutch government who were noncommittal about the idea, and then to Dr. Chaim Weizmann, the first President of Israel and the most intelligent and influential of the Zionists. He rejected the idea out of hand. Because I was known to be a friend of Jim's, the charges against him were enlarged to include having favored a second Jewish homeland.

Shortly after I returned from Japan after completing the field-work for the Pacific Report of USSBS, a further issue arose on which I consulted Jim. In February 1946, Stalin made an important speech concerning the postwar policy of the USSR. In it he asserted that the USSR continued to be surrounded by potential enemies; it was essential that the USSR not only rebuild the damage that had occurred during the war but go on to build a strong defense. The buildup would require at least three five-year plans. Stalin claimed that the danger of war would continue as long as capitalism continued; and, echoing Lenin's theories of imperialism, argued that capitalist countries were bound to fight with each other over the control of markets and the Soviet Union could well become involved contrary to its will. The USSR would need to have a posture so strong that it could deal with any contingency.

I considered this speech to be a delayed declaration of war against the United States, which Stalin had identified as the Soviet Union's principal long-term enemy. I went to see Jim to ask whether he agreed with my analysis of Stalin's speech. He did. I asked how we should go about obtaining adequate recognition in the government of the long-term problem we faced in dealing with the Soviet Union. Jim surprised me by asserting that the main problem in achieving such a consensus was my "friend" Dean Acheson. He suggested I go over to the State Department and talk to Dean who, he said, was the heart of the problem.

I had known Dean Acheson for many years. His senior law partner before he entered the State Department, Edward Burl-ing, for many years was a friend of my father. I went to Dean's office and explained my concerns to him. He was unsympathet-ic. At that time Acheson was one of the most forceful voices in Washington advocating a policy of doing everything we could to continue into peacetime the wartime alliance among Britain, the Soviet Union, and ourselves. Dean virtually threw me out of his office. It was not until late 1946 and early 1947 that Acheson was convinced by events to switch policy sides and urge that the U.S. take the lead in standing up to the Moscow brand of communism.

In the meantime, Forrestal had strongly supported Averell Harriman, our Ambassador to Moscow, who, at that time, was convinced that the Soviet Union was going to be the great threat to the West in the postwar era. Later, Jim met and encouraged George Kennan who had been serving in our embassy in Moscow when he wrote the Long Telegram that laid out the rationale for the policy of containment.

In the spring of 1946, Forrestal described to me the troubles the Navy was having putting together a carrier task force to go on a training mission from San Francisco to Adak in the Aleutians. The task force was to consist of one carrier, a cruiser, and a few destroyers. To assemble reasonably competent crews to man these ships had fully exhausted the trained manpower resources of the Navy. The best sailors had already disappeared into civilian life within a few months after the Japanese surrender: the crews manning the engine rooms of ships had all had years of service; they were in great demand by the private shipping lines whose business was booming in the postwar economic recovery. Within a few months, the U.S. Navy was reduced from the most powerful military organization in the world to close to zero military effectiveness.

The problems of the force reduction took an increasing toll upon Jim and upon his relationship with President Truman, who in 1947 appointed Jim the first Secretary of Defense. Even after his bold decision in February of 1947 to adopt the policy of containment, with all its political consequences, the President harbored grave doubts about any rise in the greatly reduced defense budget ceilings already in place. Jim was faced with fulfilling a new defense plan with tightly restricted resources, and the President consistently denied his frequent appeals for relief.

The growing alienation between Forrestal and Truman moved from disagreement over defense matters into problems of practical politics. During the war years, after Roosevelt's decision to seek bipartisan support for his foreign and defense policies, it had become customary for cabinet officials such as the Secretary of State and what is now the Secretary of Defense not to involve themselves in party politics during election campaigns. Jim thought he should continue the practice, but President Truman and his Democratic political associates were not sympathetic to Forrestal's detachedness from the campaign. Furthermore, there were rumors that Jim had met with the Republican candidate Tom Dewey.

Challenges to Forrestal's position as Secretary of Defense began to emerge. Louis Johnson, in charge of fundraising for Truman's campaign, used his close connections with the President to try and replace Jim as secretary. Stuart Symington, long a personal friend of Forrestal and then the first Secretary of the Air Force, reporting directly to Jim, cultivated a close political relationship to the President and began to take positions contrary to Jim's guidance. Symington's disloyalty struck deep: Jim had helped Stuart establish a new career when Symington's original company, the Rustless Iron & Steel Company of Baltimore, went into bankruptcy.

In his last months, Jim's greatest resentment was over what he considered such disloyalty and betrayal among his closest friends. Besides Symington, there was Arthur Krock, a former classmate at Princeton who had tutored Jim in the ways and politics of Washington when Forrestal arrived in 1940. Arthur enjoyed playing kingmaker in Washington and decided to support Louis Johnson for Secretary of Defense, should Truman win the 1948 election. The defection of Krock, who overtly supported Johnson, hurt Jim deeply.

Jim felt increasingly alone in his responsibility for American interests in the face of what he considered the implacable hostility of Moscow and his inability to secure enough support to strengthen the declining U. S. military capabilities. His alienation from the president, and Truman's unbending loyalty to the Zionist cause, caused him to become depressed and introverted.

The combination of the collapse of his public career and the desertion of friends devastated Forrestal. His professional career, even in his Wall Street days, was his principal source of inner satisfaction. Jim had always shied from close personal relationships and had never really been very close even to his wife. His difficult marriage remained a thorn in his side. Jim's depression began to wear on him, and in early 1949 friends persuaded him to take a rest at Hobe Sound in Florida. I hoped the rest would return Jim's spirits and confidence.

I had to leave for Paris that spring to attend a conference with the Soviets in the aftermath of the Berlin Blockade. While there, I received word that my old friend and mentor had committed suicide. I keenly regretted that I had not been able to be with him in his final days.

As was the case with other historical figures who demonstrated extraordinary strength of will in persistently and single-mindedly pursuing their objectives, Jim Forrestal's rise to power and influence sprang from passion. From the standpoint of the theory and practice of politics, the single-minded will of a great leader is crucially important but it is not absolute; its role depends on the character of the leader and the political strategic situation in which his opportunities arise.

Lenin, for example, was persistent and undeviating in his determination to impose his plan for the triumph of Marxism-Leninism worldwide. His persistence rose from the depth and universality of his hatred. He hated not only the Czar but all the institutions of Russian society. He believed they all had to be swept away, including not only the government, the bureaucracy, the military, and the Church, but Russia itself. He hated the very idea of nationality, of ethnicity, of patriotism; they were all alien and dangerous to his idea of the worldwide dominance of a leadership elite, preferably obedient to him, which would represent the true class interests of the world proletariat. Whenever he had doubts about his past course or present decisions, the depth and breadth of this almost universal hatred brought him back to his dedication to the execution of his plan for almost universal destruction.

Hitler also showed enormous dedication to his idea, to his objective. But his hatreds were, to some extent, synthetic, with a passion vented on convenient targets. At one point he is reported to have said that if the Jews had not existed it would have been necessary to invent them. He was particularly ambivalent about England. His doctrine centered on race and he saw little distinction between the Germans and Anglo-Saxons. What he desired was an alliance with England, which, if possible, would have freed him to turn German energies single-mindedly against the Russians. But Hitler's political strategic situation and the character of his goals prevented his success. When he let England escape what appeared to be a position of great weakness after Dunkirk, his opportunity to divide and conquer his enemies, one by one, was lost.

Originally, I had thought Forrestal illustrated the paradigm of a man dedicated to successful action for its own sake, not for any higher purpose; I thought he would have been equally happy to have been an editor of a liberal publication (at Princeton he had been editor of the *Daily Princetonian*) or as an athlete, had either of those careers offered an opportunity as great as that offered by Wall Street in the 1920s. But as I came to know him, it became evident that Forrestal's dedication to success in his chosen career came to outweigh all other loyalties. It outweighed his loyalties to his siblings, his wife, and his children. With great psychological trauma he broke with his Catholic faith although he never renounced it. In politics he was a Democrat, but, had it been useful to what he was trying to get done, he would have joined the Republicans.

Later, I came to understand that Jim's single-minded dedication to success was in part inconsistent with his natural instincts and character, and that he often had to fight his emotions when he had to take action. Those instincts included being sympathetic and helpful to his friends and associates. It was easy for him to make friends. It was to past friends and associates that he looked when building the new organizations needed in the changed, postwar world. From time to time, I would compare Forrestal to Clarence Dillon. Dillon also had an indomitable will when in an action mode, but he would alternate between an analytical and an action mode. When he was in an analytical mode he would examine all alternatives in a wholly objective manner. When he had made up his mind what the situation was, what the best of the alternatives for action was, and had decided he would follow that course, he would close his mind to further objective weighing of alternatives. At that point, he would act with single-minded determination.

Forrestal's will for personal success appears originally to have been amorphous; it might have been channelled into any of several different possible careers. His need was to get away both from his mother's ambition that he become a Catholic priest and also from his father's easy Irish bonhomie. Once he found a satisfying career in Wall Street he was able totally to sublimate his will to success into his career as an investment banker. It took precedence over his family, his ties to his church, and the more sensitive parts of his character.

When in 1940 he arrived in Washington, he was immediately caught up into affairs of far wider scope and significance. During the war and the immediate postwar years, he made a unique contribution both to the allied military victory and to the transformation of the United States into the world's only true superpower. It is hardly surprising that his mind collapsed after the President and his earlier friends Arthur Krock and Stuart Symington turned against him, and while he was being vilified by Drew Pearson, Walter Winchell, Bartley Crum, and the whole panoply of our most vigorous character assassins. That he held out so long is what is notable. Will, courage and persistence are important virtues in the conduct of politics.

7

WILL CLAYTON: VIRTUE AND COMPETENCE

In the summer of 1940, Jim Forrestal worked with a cabinet level group on the draft of the executive order creating the Office of the Coordinator of Inter-American Affairs. The order provided for the creation of such an office reporting directly to the President but made no recommendation as to who that coordinator should be. Jim had prepared a list for President Roosevelt of the names of some twenty men he thought competent to run the organization. Heading the list was William L. "Will" Clayton of Houston, founder of Anderson, Clayton & Co., with numerous connections in Latin America. Others on the list included Ferdinand Eberstadt, a brilliant and hard-driving lawyer and financier who at one time had been a partner in Dillon, Read & Co.; Nelson Rockefeller, who had recently sent a memo to Harry Hopkins recommending improved cultural and political relations with Latin America; as well as John Hay "Jock" Whitney, Juan Trippe, and a number of others.

I did not personally know Clayton but Forrestal thought him to be first class. He was raised in Jackson, Tennessee, where his father had failed as a small-scale railroad construction contractor. Because of his family's economic hardships, Clayton left school at the age of twelve and found a job at the courthouse at Jackson. From that time on he worked long hours with extreme concentration both to help support his family and to continue his education on the side. He decided to learn shorthand in order to shorten the time he had to devote to his job as a court reporter, setting aside four dollars of his ten-dollars-a-month salary to pay the former deputy clerk for lessons at night. Clayton also continued his school studies under the direct supervision of the school superintendent. At the age of fifteen he was offered a job in St. Louis earning $65 a month and left Jackson after finishing only the eighth grade. From then on he taught himself.[1]

At the age of twenty-four, Clayton, his brother-in-law Frank Anderson, and Frank's brother Monroe each put up $3000 to found Anderson, Clayton & Co., cotton merchants in Oklahoma City. They quickly became successful locally and then spread their business across the United States and the leading commodity trading centers of the world.

Early in his life, Will met, and after a difficult five-year courtship married, the belle of Clinton, Kentucky, Sue Vaughan. Alben Barkley, who later became Truman's Vice President, had also been a suitor.[2]

"Miss Sue," as she was widely known, expected continuous attention and adoration. Her gaiety and sharp wit may have been a necessary offset to Will's seriousness and determination. Later, when I came to know her well, I found her somewhat of a

---

[1]   For an excellent account of Clayton's life and contributions through public service, see Gregory A. Fossedal, *Our Finest Hour: Will Clayton, the Marshall Plan and the Triumph of Democracy* (Stanford: Hoover Institution Press, 1993); also see Ellen Clayton Garwood, *Will Clayton: A Short Biography* (Austin: University of Texas Press, 1958).

[2]   Fossedal, p. 18.

trial. But I was told that by that time she was suffering from an illness that had robbed her of her natural gaiety.

When Jim Forrestal took his list of names to President Roosevelt for him to select someone to head the new office, the President proved reluctant to appoint Clayton. Clayton, he said, had contributed $25,000 to the Republican Party. Roosevelt was also reluctant to approve Eberstadt, whom he found "too prickly." When he got to the name of Nelson Rockefeller, he was more sympathetic; he commented that though a Republican, Nelson had contributed $25,000 to his campaign fund.

Forrestal objected that Nelson was too self-centered and erratic to be counted on. He suggested that, if the President chose Nelson, he should select Will Clayton to be Rockefeller's deputy to give the organization the solidity and competence that Nelson lacked. Roosevelt thought a minute and reflected that maybe that would be all right; while Will had contributed $25,000 to the Republicans, Miss Sue had contributed $10,000 to his campaign. That was how the matter was settled, at least for the short-run.[3]

After a few months as deputy to Nelson Rockefeller, Jesse Jones, head of the Reconstruction Finance Corporation, persuaded Clayton to become deputy Federal Loan Administrator and vice president of the Export-Import Bank. In February 1942, President Roosevelt personally asked Will to become Assistant Secretary of Commerce and director of the foreign operations of the RFC. Clayton carried out these various responsibilities with great effectiveness and skill.

Before Pearl Harbor and during the early months thereafter, the principal task of the United States was to rapidly mobilize its

---

[3]   ibid., p. 69.

enormous economic potential, not only to equip our own forces but also those of the British, including Canada, and of the USSR. There were shortages everywhere: in industrial facilities, in trained manpower, in critical raw materials, and in in transportation, particularly shipping. The most critical shortages of materials were of specific metals, particularly those on which we and the British had been largely or wholly dependent upon imports from abroad.

To deal with the procurement of these critical raw materials, Jones and Clayton used the broad powers and financial resources of the Federal Loan Agency to get the task off to a fast start. They created several specialized, government-owned corporations as subsidiaries of the agency. These included the Metals Reserve Company, the Rubber Reserve Company, the U.S. Commercial Company, and a number of others. Each had its own management and board of directors and could borrow funds from the Federal Loan Agency if needed.

Will was widely known and respected in the world of business, and he personally recruited highly competent men to run this complex organization. I worked with many of these men and came to know them well, particularly those who ran the Metals Reserve Company and the U.S. Commercial Company. Clayton was an ever-present aura and influence, but I remember few instances in which he personally intervened in a negotiation or a decision. He had mastered the art of building an organization and then delegating full responsibility to those in charge of its relevant parts.

In the spring of 1942, Henry Wallace, then my boss, had transferred the focus of his ire from Cordell Hull and the State Department, whom he considered too conservative, to Jones and the RFC. As head of the Board of Economic Warfare (BEW),

Wallace insisted that he have an important voice in all foreign economic transactions. At that time, one of BEW's primary functions was to control and facilitate the importation of strategic materials. I was in charge of the metals and minerals branch of that organization, and was responsible for representing BEW views on overseas procurement actions by the Metals Reserve Company; I thought they were doing an excellent job.

Wallace succeeded, however, in getting President Roosevelt to change the rules of the game. The President signed an executive order transferring the authority to negotiate contracts for overseas procurement from the RFC to the BEW. The move was a surprise to me; I learned of it from *The New York Times*. I checked with my immediate superior, Morris Rosenthal, who merely said to get on with the expanded job.

After leaving Rosenthal, I immediately telephoned the president of the Metals Reserve Company, Temple Bridgeman, and invited him to lunch. Bridgeman was an admirable man, much older than I. He had been a senior partner in Guggenheim Brothers, an important private firm in the metals business. Here was another man who knew how to build a large, efficient organization and surround himself with a competent staff. I did not need to explain to him that I had nothing to do with the new executive order. I asked him for his advice and help in getting organized to take on much of what had been his responsibilities and he gracefully responded. He suggested names of men to recruit and was frank in telling me what he thought were my shortcomings in tackling the expanded management responsibilities of my new job.

Bridgeman recognized that I seemed more interested in dealing with the substance of difficult and complicated issues than in administration; I had no experience in running even a medium-sized organization and appeared to have little instinctive feel for doing so. It would require great self-discipline on my part, he said, to prevent my interfering in, or even taking over, the more difficult problems in the designated responsibilities of my subordinates. Perhaps I was justified in my natural confidence that I could deal with the more difficult substantive problems better than they, but I would destroy the organization if I acted on that confidence. Bridgeman recommended that I spend at least half of my time on administration—in the hiring, supervising, promoting or firing of people—and no more than half on the substantive aspects of the issues involved.

Will Clayton brought high standards and good people to important government work, and Bridgeman was typical of the executives he had assembled. It was they who made the American wartime productive effort work with unparalleled speed and effectiveness and a minimum of bureaucratic infighting.

Clayton's own practical, direct approach to problems reflected his style of operation. He thought it a waste of time to try to get factual information from people at senior levels in an organization; they would inevitably strive to obtain the information through a long chain of subordinates, each of whom would give it some twist of their own. If one really wanted to get the facts he thought it best to go directly to the man most likely to know—no matter at what level.

Once, early in the war, when I found myself dealing with the procurement of strategic commodities, a problem arose with respect to a shortage of long staple cotton, which was used to make gun cotton, an important explosive. An old high school friend from Chicago, Jim Baker, was a cotton specialist at the State Department, working at a relatively low-ranking level. One day he telephoned me to ask whether I had ever heard of a man named Clayton. I said I had and asked why. He told me a distinguished older-looking gentleman had that morning knocked on his door in the basement of the State Department building asking about cotton. It turned out that Clayton had simply looked into the State Department directory to identify its expert in cotton and decided from his job description that Baker was the man who should know everything the department knew about long staple cotton.

Having been appointed Assistant Secretary of State for Economic Affairs in 1944, Clayton was promoted in 1946 to Undersecretary of State for Economic Affairs. At that time the economic side of the State Department had the most competent economic staff in the government—even, I believe, in the world. It had inherited not only the economists who had worked in the State Department in the later days of the war, including Emilio G. Collado and Jacob Viner, but had also absorbed most of the competent economists who had worked for Lend-Lease, the BEW, and subsequently, the Foreign Economic Administration.

Shortly after Clayton became Undersecretary, an international meeting to begin work on a General Agreement on Tariffs and Trade (GATT) was scheduled to get under way in Geneva. Clair Wilcox, the head of the State Department's Office of International Trade Policy, was to represent the United States. Clayton considered the economic recovery of Europe to be his highest immediate priority, but in the long run a worldwide reduction in trade barriers would be the key to world economic growth and the relief of economic tensions that could otherwise tear the world apart and jeopardize the chances for an enduring peace.

He, therefore, wanted to give Clair freedom to stay away from Washington for as long as success in his task required. He asked me whether I would become Clair's deputy and take over his Washington duties until he returned. I agreed.

Clayton was three echelons senior to me in the State Department hierarchy, so I initially saw relatively little of him, but his energy, courtesy, and decisiveness dominated our part of the department. In March of 1947 Clayton wrote out a memorandum to Secretary of State Marshall, who was abroad at the time, regarding how the U.S. should take action in Europe to ensure both the stability of the liberated countries and U.S. interests. In the memorandum, Clayton pointed out that "world leadership was fast slipping from England's competent but weak hands." If the Soviets took charge there would almost certainly be war within the next decade; if the United States took the lead, we could almost certainly avert war. Furthermore, in every country of the Eastern Hemisphere and most of those in the Western Hemisphere, the Soviets were "boring from within." Several nations whose integrity were vital to American interests and security were threatened.[4]

Clayton told Marshall that he would discuss with the Congress a program of aid to Greece and Turkey, for if they succumbed the whole of the Middle East would be lost. On Marshall's return, he would propose to him a joint statement by the President and the Secretary of State to the Congress and the American people to spell out the whole truth of the situation and the actions necessary to deal with it.

Clayton recommended that this statement to Congress should include evidence of the Soviet campaign to undermine the in-

---

[4]   The text of the memorandum is included in Fossedal, p. 217.

Christian A. Herter,
congressman, Secretary of State,
and co-founder of the School
of Advanced International
Studies.
Courtesy of SAIS Archives.

Charles Burton Marshall, member
of the State Department Policy
Planning Staff and, later, Professor
of International Politics at SAIS.
Courtesty of System Planning Corporation.

Rev. John Courtney Murray, S.J., professor of theology at Woodstock College, Maryland, and wise counsel, in 1966. UPI/Bettmann.

Nitze (left) with Soviet envoy Yuli Kvitsinsky during the INF negotiations in Geneva, March 1983.

Courtesy of Jean Zbinden.

James V. Forrestal,
Secretary of Defense
and partner at Dillon,
Read, in 1949.
UPI/Bettmann.

William Clayton, Undersecretary of State for Economic Affairs, in 1948.
UPI/Bettmann.

Ambassador George F. Kennan (left), director of the first policy planning staff and, later, ambassador to the Soviet Union and Yugoslavia, with Nitze in Salzburg, Austria, summer 1970. Author's collection.

Secretary of State staff meeting, 1950. *From left:* Edward W. Barrett, Willard L. Thorp, John E. Peurifoy, James E. Webb, Dean Acheson, Dean Rusk, Paul H. Nitze, Jack K. McFall, and William J. McWilliams. UPI/Bettmann.

Dean Acheson (right), Secretary of State, with President Harry S Truman in 1950.
UPI/Bettmann.

President Harry S Truman (left) with Secretary of State George C. Marshall, 1948.
UPI/Bettmann.

Nitze greets Soviet President Mikhail S. Gorbachev (left) at a White House dinner in Gorbachev's honor during the Washington Summit, December 1987. President Reagan looks on. Courtesy of the Ronald Reagan Presidential Library.

From left: Secretary of State George P. Shultz, Nitze, and President Reagan in the Oval Office, December 1984. Courtesy of the Ronald Reagan Presidential Library.

tegrity and independence of other nations. How, "feeding on hunger, economic misery and frustration these attacks had already been successful in some of the liberated countries, and that there was grave danger that they would be successful in others." It should also emphasize that American and world security and interests demanded that "the United States take prompt and effective action to assist certain of these gravely threatened countries. Such assistance should take the form not only of financial aid, but of technical and administrative assistance as well." Clayton also proposed that the administration should ask Congress to create a Council of National Defense and to appropriate $5 billion for use by the Council to assist sovereign countries in preserving their integrity and independence.[5]

In later memoranda, Clayton outlined the amounts the plan would require overall year by year, how the money should be divided among the principal recipients, the United Kingdom, France, Italy, Western Germany, and other countries, and how these amounts related to projected balance of payments deficits and surpluses. The most imaginative and constructive of his proposals was that the local currency counterpart of our aid (the sums they could charge in their own currency to their own citizens or agencies for the materials or services made available) should be deposited with international trustees with restrictions upon its use. In no case should any of these funds go into the budget of that country. The potential inflationary impact of these expenditures would thus be offset and controlled.[6]

In these memoranda, Clayton was laying out the major facets of what would become the Marshall Plan. A tremendous

---

[5]   Fossedal, p. 218.

[6]   Garwood, p. 124.

amount of work by others in Europe and in the United States was necessary to refine the program and to have the funds authorized, appropriated, and effectively administered. But Clayton brilliantly laid out its essential outlines in advance.

That Clayton's role in these matters was generally overlooked is not too surprising. He spent little, if any, time with the press. At one stage, when Clayton was in Europe getting a firsthand understanding of what was happening economically and politically in each country, Joe Alsop and I had supper together just before Alsop was to catch a plane to Europe. Joe protested that Clayton was taking insufficient interest in what was going on over there. In rebutting those unjustified charges I referred to Clayton's attitudes as reported in the cables he was sending back to Washington.

That night, after I had left him, Joe wrote a column entitled "The Clayton Cables." It appeared a day later, after he had left for Europe. I read it with horror. There was certain to be an investigation as to who had leaked the substance of the cables to Joe; I would have to acknowledge that it had been I. When I went to Acheson's small morning staff meeting, he opened the discussion by asking us whether we had read Joe's article. Before anyone could answer, Acheson said that it was the most helpful thing that could have happened; the public should know how helpful Will Clayton was being. Clayton would never say anything about it himself. I was off the hook.

Shortly thereafter I was made deputy assistant secretary of state for economic affairs and worked much more directly with Will Clayton; in fact, I soon became his principal staff assistant, a position I still held when he resigned, under pressure from his wife, to return to Houston.

All those associated in any way with Will Clayton during

World War II and the crucial years immediately thereafter knew themselves to have had rare good fortune. They had known a man of true virtue and practical wisdom. He combined all the virtues of a man, a husband, a father, a citizen, and a public servant: he was highly competent and immensely hard-working, seeking no honors, publicity, or high position for himself. He believed in this country and its people and also knew the world and its needs.

8

GEORGE KENNAN AND POLICY PLANNING: THE NEXUS BETWEEN THEORY AND PRACTICE

I t was only by accident that I first met George Kennan. On a crowded train from New York to Washington in late July of 1943, I wandered into the dining car for lunch and found a table for two occupied by a distinguished-looking gentleman, somewhat older than I. I sat down opposite him and we introduced ourselves. The time passed quickly as the train made its way toward Washington. As we became engrossed in conversation, I very quickly discovered not only many shared interests, but that my dining partner was charming, witty, and urbane.

He described a Fourth of July celebration he had given at the U.S. Ambassador's residence in the countryside outside of Lisbon while the Ambassador was away. He had invited the appropriate people from the Lisbon diplomatic corps and then entertained them with an exhibition of fireworks. These included some fairly long-range rockets. One or two of them had crossed a gully dividing the American property from a Portuguese neighbor's property on the other side. It was hot and extremely dry on that Fourth of July, and the rockets ignited a small forest fire. George mobilized the entire group at his luncheon and led them down into the gully with jugs of water, brooms, and other devices to put out the flames. They finally doused them and emerged covered with soot and scratches at the Portuguese house on the other side. He found the episode hilarious.

It was only after this introduction that he told me why he was on his way to Washington. He was going there to receive guidance from the White House on negotiating base rights for U.S. Air Force planes in the Azores—rights the United States even then thought might be necessary in the event of a confrontation with the USSR.

In March of 1947, General George C. Marshall, then Secretary of State, returned from a thoroughly unproductive meeting of foreign ministers in Moscow. Molotov and Stalin had proved to be adamantly unresponsive to the American, British, and French diplomats, and Marshall believed he had not been adequately prepared by his State Department staff. He asked Acheson to have a Policy Planning Staff created that would concentrate on analyzing and making recommendations on upcoming strategic issues, particularly those concerning the USSR. To head the projected staff, Acheson selected George Kennan who, at that time, was serving at the newly established National War College in Washington. George asked that I serve as his deputy, but Acheson turned his proposal down on the grounds that my background was that of a Wall Street entrepreneur, not that of a long-range thinker.

George had by this time written two important and influential papers; one was the Long Telegram that was subsequently published in 1947 in *Foreign Affairs* under the pseudonym of X. Called "The Sources of Soviet Conduct."[1] It was a penetrating

---

[1]   X (George F. Kennan), "The Sources of Soviet Conduct." *Foreign Affairs* (July 1947) 25:566–582.

analysis of the nature of Marxist/Leninist doctrine, its transformation into Stalinism, the actions to be expected from such a regime, and the gains it was making in expanding its power and influence, particularly in Central Europe. It also emphasized the necessity that Stalinist expansionism be "contained." George concluded with the forecast that, if that expansionism could be contained for a sufficiently long period of time, the Soviet conspiracy would eventually look inward into what was happening within the Soviet Union and address itself to its internal problems rather than pursue further expansion.

The second Kennan paper was drafted under his guidance by the State, War, Navy Coordinating Committee (SWNCC) in 1948. Given the designation NSC-20/4 after being submitted to the National Security Council, it translated into U.S. policy terms the line of thought in the Long Telegram. I was impressed by Kennan's sensitivity and insight. It seemed evident that he had a deep understanding and love of Russian culture and correctly grasped that Leninist/Stalinist doctrine and action were as alien and hostile to Russian culture as they were to Western culture as a whole.

George Kennan tended to look upon diplomacy as the queen of the policy disciplines, having its origins in early Western culture and its flowering in the days of Metternich and the worldwide preeminence of European statesmen and diplomats. He considered those statesmen to have been members of a small elite group who understood the special rules of the European diplomatic code: namely, that the survival of no European state should be threatened, and if any European state threatened to become dominant, the others should coalesce against the potentially dominant one to support the maintenance of a balance of power. The domestic politics of the individual states might be, and often were, at variance with these demands of diplomacy. If this happened, the statesmen-diplomats should hold out against such lack of understanding of the rules of the game. As the classical Greeks considered all nonGreeks to be barbarians, so the exploitation by European regimes of nonEuropeans was not frowned upon and generally was admired.

George's admiration of European diplomacy led him to focus his attention in the immediate postwar years upon the political and economic recovery of Europe. As an economist, I tended to look at those same economic problems with less regional bias, favoring a global view rather than a regional one. I thought the figures showed the world requiring an average of about $5 billion a year of U.S. economic aid over the five years beginning with 1947; I also believed that this aid should be given where its need and efficacy would be the greatest. But when Will Clayton and Dean Acheson backed George's position of focusing on Europe, I readily concurred; it was more important to get the program under way promptly than to waste time over optimizing its distribution.

Later in 1949, when the Soviets lifted their blockade of Berlin in response to our airlift of coal and supplies, the USSR demanded a meeting of the U.S., Soviet, British and French Foreign Ministers at the Palais Rose in Paris. Chip Bohlen was given the task of preparing the preliminary papers on the political issues for the U.S. delegation, and I was directed to deal with the economic papers.

There soon developed an important difference of opinion between Chip Bohlen and George Kennan as to what opening ploy to expect from the Soviet side. We all thought it must be new and dramatic to be commensurate with the importance the Soviets seemed to have attached to the meeting. George thought they might propose the withdrawal of all allied forces, including all Soviet as well as Western forces, from Germany—including Berlin. Chip was confident they would not remove theirs, that they were too worried about a possible revival of German military capabilities to take such a chance. It was my view that, in any case, we ought to have a position prepared in advance in the event the Soviets did call for a mutual force withdrawal.

As a result, George Kennan and I prepared what became known as "Plan A." It drew heavily upon an earlier effort of George's to move toward a unified Germany through a mutual withdrawal of military forces. Under Plan A we would gradually remove all our military forces from Germany except for a small contingent securing for us access to the port of Bremerhaven. The Allies would gradually turn over political authority in Berlin and Germany to German political institutions, whose decisions the Allies could veto only by unanimous agreement.

The day before the formal meeting opened, General V. I. Chuikov, the Soviet High Commissioner in East Germany, made it clear the Soviets had no intentions of removing any of their forces from Germany at that time. Plan A was, therefore, dead. We fell back to Plan B, which contemplated no withdrawal of military forces from Germany.

During those weeks, George and I had worked together smoothly and, I thought, effectively. He asked me whether I would leave the economic side of the Department and become Deputy Director of the Policy Planning Staff. I was interested. Earlier, Acheson had vetoed the proposal, but now he assented.

In the fall of 1949, word came to us that the analysis of air samples floating east from over Russia contained nuclear particles that could only have come from an atmospheric burst of an atomic device. It was evident that our nuclear monopoly shortly would be a thing of the past. Acheson called Kennan and me into his office and asked that over the weekend we each draft a paper proposing what the U.S. reaction should be to this event. We came to very different conclusions.

George's paper expressed horror at the consequences of a competition between the United States and the Soviet Union to build such weapons. The U.S. was a great country, he thought, but we had many problems: racial inequality, inadequate public education, and maldistribution of wealth. In essence, he held that moral leadership was of far greater importance than superiority in the destructiveness of weapons. He recommended that the U.S. adopt a policy of unilateral nuclear disarmament.

My paper argued we could now expect that the Soviets would focus their efforts fully to offset and counter our nuclear capabilities. They had the resources and skills to do so. As they approached—even if only roughly—nuclear equality with us, their evident nonnuclear military superiority on the Eurasian landmass would become decisive unless we took steps to counter it. To do so, we needed to increase our conventional military capabilities and to assist a network of allies also to increase theirs. It would take us many years to achieve a rough equality in nonnuclear forces. To extend the time available to do so, we should continue to work on developing our nuclear capability even though the net contribution it could make to the support of our foreign policy over the years would asymptotically approach zero.

Acheson's views corresponded much more closely to mine than to George's. George, during the next few weeks, wrote an expanded and refined paper and delivered it to Acheson. Having done so, he considered his task completed. For some time he had been eager to return to academia, and he informed Acheson at the end of August 1950 that he wished a year's leave of absence to become a visiting scholar at Princeton's Institute for Advanced Study, then headed by J. Robert Oppenheimer. I then took over as director of the Policy Planning Staff, effective January 1, 1950.

From time to time during the period that I served as his deputy, George and I discussed the magnitude of U.S. conventional forces necessary to implement the policy of containing Soviet military expansionism. It was his view that two high-quality marine divisions, with the Navy support necessary to put them ashore where needed, would be fully adequate to accomplish the task. From the work we of the U.S. Strategic Bombing Survey had done three years earlier, it appeared to me that the requirement was indeterminate and might, depending on the circumstances, be many times what George was estimating.

On that issue, I found that Bohlen's and Kennan's views were relatively close together and radically different from mine. Chip Bohlen protested to Dean Acheson that in our draft of what became NSC-68 we were overestimating both the probability of further Moscow-inspired military aggression and the extent of Soviet/Chinese military capabilities. After an extended discussion, Chip was unable to persuade Acheson to overrule us. In George's later writings he also argues that NSC-68 erred both in judging Soviet intentions and in estimating its military capabilities. Shortly thereafter, the Soviet-backed surprise attack by North Korea into South Korea, and the extent of the U.S. and allied buildup required to deal with it, were widely thought to have confirmed the judgments expressed in NSC-68.

There remained some doubt as to whether Mao or Khrushchev had more vigorously promoted and backed the attack. But there could be no doubt that a communist-directed military attack had taken place and that throwing it back had been a close run thing. Our annual defense appropriations went from $13 billion to $50 billion in the course of one year.

Even though on leave from the government, Kennan continued to have some role in U.S./Soviet affairs. A year or so later, in May 1951, I received a telephone call from Andrew Corry, a foreign service officer working with the U.S. Delegation to the United Nations in New York. He said he had had a strange conversation with Semen K. Tsarapkin, a member of the Soviet Delegation to the U.N. After a long and extended denunciation of the United States, the Soviet diplomat appeared to ask whether Corry thought the United States might be interested in an armistice in Korea. I asked Corry to fly down to Washington immediately.

When he arrived, C. B. Marshall and I saw him and took him in to see Acheson. Acheson explained that we should not appear anxious for an armistice. We should wait for the Soviets to show a more definite interest first. We decided to ask George Kennan, who knew well Jacob A. Malik, Tsarapkin's boss and head of the Soviet U.N. delegation, to see Malik and inquire, as a friend of both sides, whether Moscow had any interest in exploring the idea of an armistice. George approached Malik with the question. Malik responded that he did not know, but would inquire in Moscow, since it happened he was on his way there the next morning. A few weeks later, with no prior notice to us, Malik made a speech at the United Nations proposing the prompt initiation of armistice negotiations.

In September of 1951, George requested an additional year's leave and then appointment to a foreign post. A few months later, Alan Kirk, the U.S. Ambassador to Moscow, told Washington he wished to be relieved after more than two years of frustrating work there. Acheson and Truman offered the position to

Kennan. George was reluctant, but Chip Bohlen persuaded him to accept the job. It proved a difficult and extremely taxing assignment. George attempted to establish some basis for useful dialogue with the Soviets but he found it impossible. Their espionage was all-pervasive; their press was flooded with lies, including charges of U.S. torture and brutality in Korea.

One of the few people in Moscow with whom Kennan could have an intelligent exchange of views, outside of his immediate staff, was the British Ambassador, an experienced diplomat named Sir Alvary Gascoigne. Gascoigne had served in a number of diplomatic posts and had been given the post at Moscow as an appropriate reward for a long and distinguished career. Gascoigne liked to walk with his two large dogs from the British Embassy along the river. The KGB had three of their agents walk directly behind him and one in front. George considered this treatment of a distinguished diplomat to be an insult to the diplomatic profession. Obviously, he too was subject to similar treatment. Increasingly, he began to take personally Soviet rudeness, espionage, and vilification of the West and of the U.S. in particular. These seemed to be directed not just against an improvement of diplomatic relations between the U.S. and the USSR, but against George's position on every issue of policy. He believed in the unification of Germany, a Korean ceasefire and armistice, and demilitarization rather than increasing U.S. and Soviet militarization. The Soviets were not only against all those positions, they did not even wish to talk to him about them. They were against diplomacy itself.

George also had continuing problems in his relations with Washington. He had left for Moscow with no instructions from Truman and little guidance from Acheson other than to take no initiatives that might upset European economic and political integration. In the few months he was in Moscow his relations with Washington did not improve. Kennan felt lonely and desperately unhappy. He also worried deeply about the McCarthyite attacks on John Paton Davies, J. Robert Oppenheimer, and Charlie Thayer, and other of his close friends in Washington.

In September of 1952, when Kennan's plane stopped at Berlin en route to London, a crowd of reporters surrounded him. One of them asked the Ambassador about life in Moscow. He answered that it was worse than if Moscow had been under the Nazis. The Soviet government denounced him and shortly thereafter declared him to be persona non grata.

That week I was staying at the house of Julius Holmes, the second in command at our Embassy in London. When George arrived, he also was invited to stay there. I believe I was the first American policy official to see George after his Berlin press conference. He told me he had not intended to accuse the Soviets of being worse than the Nazis, but when the press put him in a position where he either had to be hypocritical—in effect to lie—he couldn't bring himself to do so. Then, he spelled out his deep revulsion at the way the Soviets had treated Ambassador Gascoigne, their contempt for diplomacy, and his resentment at their overwhelming persistence in perversion of the media and in espionage.

About the same time, it was discovered that the Soviets had implanted in the Great Seal of the United States that hung in George's personal office in Spaso House in Moscow a device that could broadcast to the KGB all conversations in his office, including his dictation of top-secret telegrams to the President and the Secretary of State. The device had no wires or magnetic tape and required no batteries, so the debugging equipment of those days could not find it. A wideband American receiver had by accident hit the right frequency and intercepted what the device was rebroadcasting; it was George's voice dictating to his secretary.

Later, when George returned to Washington he saw C.B. Marshall who had also, at one time, been a member of the State Department's Policy Planning Staff. What he told C.B. differed materially from what he had told me. In that version, George had determined prior to his arrival in Berlin to announce to the press the utter horror of Soviet behavior; he argued that if he had not done so the U.S. and the world as a whole would not understand what was going on in Moscow. There can be little doubt that he was under great stress during his ambassadorship to Moscow.

In 1957, George was asked to give the Reith lectures in London, broadcast over BBC radio over six successive Sunday nights. In the first two, he announced that his recommendations in the X article were out of date. The Soviet Union's economic progress since the article's appearance in 1947 exceeded anything he had then thought possible; it was, therefore, impossible to suppose that containment by itself would result in radical change in the Soviet Union. The maximum to be hoped for from negotiations was resolution of specific problems. In the third lecture he asserted that to initiate military withdrawal from Germany by the great powers was the only way to resolve the Berlin issue and the Soviet Union's domination of Eastern Europe. In his fourth lecture he attacked the notion of deploying tactical nuclear weapons on European soil. He disapproved of the ideas advanced in Henry Kissinger's book *Nuclear Weapons and Foreign Policy*, which I also had criticized. George advocated minimum nuclear deterrence, not unilateral disarmament. He suggested that Western Europe follow the Swiss model of universal military participation in reserve forces, with little or no permanent standing army.

In Europe, Kennan's Reith lectures had a mixed response. They were widely applauded by students and opposition parties. Most of the governments in power, who had participated in the NATO decisions to build Western strength, objected strongly. Dean Acheson, who at the time was Chairman of the Democratic National Committee's Foreign Policy Advisory Council, asked me, when in Geneva, to talk to him about our mutual worries about these lectures. Both George and I were going to the Swiss city at the invitation of Louis Halle.

During a three-hour walk that George, Louis, and I took along the quay overlooking the eastern end of Lake Geneva, George dismissed any importance attached to his lectures. He had agreed to give them more or less by mistake; an assistant had prepared them for him. She had done all the writing; he hadn't had time to go over them carefully. I had the impression, however, that he had said what he wanted to say in the lectures and didn't propose to take seriously Dean's and my concerns.

In spite of our differences, George and I have always been good friends and our families remained close. From time to time, the Kennans would invite us to share a weekend at their farm near Gettysburg in Pennsylvania; sometimes, the Kennans would visit us. When George celebrated his eightieth birthday at Princeton, I believe Phyllis and I were the only Washingtonians to be invited. That evening, someone asked me how George and I continued to be such warm friends despite our frequent and well-publicized differences on national security policy. My reply was that I had never had any difference with George except on matters of substance. George's toast reflected the same thought.

But, to look at the matter more seriously, George has made an immense contribution to the world's understanding of the richness of the American character, or, as the Russians would say, of the American soul. The world viewed America as a fountain of material prosperity, and as a leader in science, technology, research, and rational thought. We had demonstrated its ability to organize and command immense military power. But people doubted our ability to see the other side of world issues and recognize America's internal tendencies toward greed, corruption, and intellectual illiteracy. George eloquently called for the renewal of American virtue and self-sacrifice, and his own life represented those virtues.

In 1993 George published a different kind of book, *Around the Cragged Hill*[2] Early in this book he states a fundamental proposition: that man—Western man at any rate—is a cracked vessel, that his psychic makeup is the scene for the interplay of contradictions between the primitive nature of his innate impulses and the more refined demands of civilized life, contradictions that destroy the integrity of his undertakings, confuse his efforts, place limits on his possibilities of achievement, and often cause one part of his personality to be the enemy of another. This seems to me to be too tragic a proposition. I believe a better way of looking at the problem is through the lens of the concept of the complementarity of opposites: that it is through the tension between opposites that truth, beauty, and life is to be found. In this context it is the tensions between man's humanity and the constraints of the cultures of which he is a part that produce the rich life that makes it worth living.

Later, having identified the major problems facing the United

[2]   Kennan, George F., *Around the Cragged Hill: A Personal and Political Philosophy* (New York: W. W. Norton, 1993).

States, Kennan concludes that they are all long-term problems rather than short-term ones. After outlining the reasons why it is difficult for either the executive branch or the legislative branch to deal objectively with long-range problems, he suggests the creation of a council of state whose task would be confined to telling the country what ought to be done in the long-term interest of the United States. It would then be up to the politicians to see what would be politically possible in the way of implementing these judgments. I fully endorse George's proposal.

George has managed to generate more respect and affection, particularly among European intellectuals and youth, than any other American working in the field of foreign policy. As for myself, most of my ideas concerning the formulation of policy have either been stimulated by him, borrowed from him, or else generated by opposition to those of his proposals I thought were impractical.

9

Dean Acheson and the Virtues and Limitations of Elegance

Looking back on Dean Acheson, I think of him primarily as a friend. That had not been true when I worked for him. Then, he was my boss and I looked up to and admired him; earlier he had disapproved of me and I of him. It was only after John Foster Dulles succeeded him as Secretary of State in January of 1953 that our relationship became wholly natural.

I first met Acheson through one of my father's best friends, Edward (Ned) Burling. Burling was a Chicago lawyer, and my father was a humanist and a scholar at the University of Chicago who seemed to have no particular knowledge of the law. At first I could not understand what brought the two together, but Ned had a clear and outreaching mind, and he and my father would talk together with great interest on many subjects.

In 1919, Ned joined Judge J. Harry Covington in Washington as a partner in a new law firm, which became Covington and Burling. In 1921, the firm asked Dean Acheson, who had been a law clerk to Justice Brandeis, to join them. Thereafter, whenever Ned asked my father to come to Washington, he would invite a number of his friends, often including Acheson, to join them for a picnic lunch on a wild piece of forest he owned on the Virginia shore of the Potomac above what is now the Beltway. In those days, I was either in school in the east or working in New York. I would come down to Washington to visit my parents when they were there. That is how I was first exposed to Acheson. He was much younger than Burling and brilliant in conversation; I was somewhat awed by him.

Acheson emerged as an important figure in my official life in 1943 after I arrived in Washington and was working for the Foreign Economic Administration (FEA) under Leo Crowley. At that time Dean was Assistant Secretary of State for Economic Affairs, a position he held until August 1945. Franklin Roosevelt did not believe in clear lines of division between the powers and responsibilities of one department or agency and those of another. He had assigned power and responsibility for action in the foreign economic field to the FEA. But the State Department had traditionally held responsibility for the formulation and execution of foreign policy, which it deemed to include foreign economic policy. State did not wish to surrender that function.

This overlapping responsibility led to conflicts between the agency and the department. At one point, the State Department directed me to use funds under the control of the FEA to buy fish caught by Icelandic fishermen that could not find a market because of the U-boat war in the waters around Iceland. I doubted the wisdom of this directive and said I would carry it out only if directed to do so in writing by Acheson. No such written directive was issued and another way was found to deal with the problem.

Acheson described his frustration with the erosion of State Department authority in the economic field during World War II in the opening chapter of his book *Present at the Creation*. He justifiably came to the opinion that I was a principal part of that problem. Furthermore, the FEA in 1943 had taken over the Lend-Lease Administration, which dealt directly with representatives of our allies on such matters. To do that work, FEA had a staff of some hundred or more people. By comparison, the State Department's Bureau of Central European Affairs, which dealt not only with the USSR but also Poland, Czechoslovakia, Yugoslavia, Hungary and Bulgaria, consisted of only three men: Chip Bohlen, Eddie Page, a former classmate of mine at Harvard, and a foreign service officer by the name of Elbridge Durbrow.

Despite the tangled lines of responsibility, Acheson accomplished much as Assistant Secretary of State and then Undersecretary from August 1945 to June 1947. He was proud of having spearheaded the work at Bretton Woods in 1944 that created the World Bank and the International Monetary Fund. Subsequently, he negotiated much of the United Nations Charter and helped get it widely accepted and ratified, even by the Soviets. However, Dean was deeply skeptical of the UN and saw in it an idealism with little practical value for solving problems. He was also suspicious of the main United Nations organization, which seemed to him to be a haven for those who wished power without responsibility and who expected high pay and honors for accepting that privilege. Its one use, in his eyes, was as an additional avenue of negotiation between East and West. Acheson hoped to continue the wartime alliance between the USSR and the West and to make it the foundation structure for postwar peace. He was fully aware of our growing political problems with Stalin's Russia but it was not easy for him to change rapidly to a new orientation of policy focused on the Soviet problem. It took some time before events convinced him that we could not work with the Soviets.

Dean left the State Department in June of 1947 and returned to semiprivate life as a lawyer, although he also served on the Hoover Commission. In January of 1949, he returned as Secretary of State under President Truman, replacing James Byrnes. As Undersecretary, Dean had witnessed Byrnes's failure to keep Truman fully advised of his negotiations with Stalin and Foreign Minister Molotov. He believed that Byrnes had erred both procedurally and substantively, and that the President had been justified in firing Byrnes. The President carried the executive branch's responsibility for the conduct of foreign policy; it was the State Department's task both to keep the President informed and to be responsive to his judgments.

Acheson greatly admired President Truman's character, and the President found invaluable Dean's unique ability to analyze problems with clarity and to express his views with precision and wit. The result was a warm working relationship between the two men. Acheson fully understood how the President's mind worked on the major issues of domestic and foreign policy and he helped his close associates in the State Department by sharing with them what they needed to know about the President's approach, so that they could be effective in their respective areas.

The four years of 1949 to 1952, ending in January 1953, were the most gloriously productive in Acheson's life. The noncommunist world desperately needed leadership. Only the United States had the resources and skills to provide that leadership and to make it effective. Acheson was fortunate in his President, and sensitive and skilled in handling the potentially difficult relationship between a United States President and his Secretary of State. He was, therefore, in a position to carry out fully what he, borrowing from the ancient Greeks, considered the ultimate opportunity: "the exercise of vital powers along the lines of excellence, in a life affording them scope."

I had joined the State Department's Policy Planning Staff in the summer of 1949 as deputy director to George Kennan. George had for some time considered returning to scholarship and academia, so he resigned from the State Department and joined J. Robert Oppenheimer at the Institute for Advanced Study at Princeton. As a consequence, on January 1, 1950, I inherited George's position as director of the State Department's Policy Planning Staff, with an office immediately adjacent to and interconnecting with Acheson's.

To be a member of the Truman-Acheson team during those creative years of 1949 to 1953 was sheer joy, and there were very few times when my judgment differed from Acheson's. I could, for instance, go to meetings with the Joint Chiefs of Staff confident that the views I expressed were consistent with both Acheson's and the President's. From time to time the Chiefs would test that assumption, and it was consistently confirmed. It was therefore possible to transact an immense amount of business with the Pentagon with little friction and no waste of time.

Acheson, like George Shultz many years later, was at his best when working with his staff. He had confidence in us, urged us on, and encouraged us to take increasing responsibility. He protected us when we were politically attacked. He did his best to keep us fully informed, generally even about his conversations with the President. It was his view that the best way to ensure care and discretion on the part of his staff and associates in their relations with the Congress and the media was to make them feel part of his and the President's team. When I would go in to see Acheson and present some new idea to him, he would listen carefully and then tell me not only whether he agreed or disagreed, but why. The only requirement was that one not waste his time; one had to have thought the point through and be succinct in presenting it.

Shortly after I had become director of the Policy Planning Staff, I told Acheson that we on the staff had reluctantly turned down an idea we thought was correct from a foreign-policy standpoint. We had turned it down because we judged there was not enough congressional support for it. Acheson said, "Congressional support is essential but judging whether it is adequate or not isn't your job; that is the President's and my job. What we want from you and the Policy Planning Staff is your considered judgment on the issue, based on national-security and foreign-policy grounds, not on the degree to which public or congressional opinion favors a given stand. The President and I are going to have to compromise, including having to make concessions to public and congressional opinion, but we don't want these concessions made twice, first by you and then by us."

Originally, I had thought Dean felt so at ease with European ideas and culture, particularly with things British, as to be uncomfortable with other cultures. He had seemed awkward with the Far East, except for Japan, suspicious not only of the Marxist-Leninists but of Russians more generally, and quite uninterested in the Third World. In the course of Acheson's years as Undersecretary and then as Secretary of State, his job exposed him to the world leaders and the diverse cultures they represented. But even toward the end of his career, I found he bubbled with wit and joy more easily with his British friends and with the Irish than with others. Perhaps this was because of Dean's close family ties to England and Ireland.

At one time I accompanied him on a strenuous trip concerned with the Soviets and Berlin. In those days transatlantic planes had to stop at Shannon, Ireland, to refuel on their way back home. We got to Shannon at midnight. Some of the local Irish dignitaries came to the plane, woke Acheson up, and asked him to accompany them to drink Irish whiskey. Acheson was delighted with the idea, was gay and entertaining, sang with them, and enjoyed the party thoroughly. I went along, but was so tired I could barely hold up my head.

One of Acheson's precepts was to head into problems, not to shy away from them, which he considered to smack of cowardice. Occasionally, this strength could cause him some anguish. When Alger Hiss was denounced by Whittaker Chambers and was under investigation by then Senator Richard Nixon, the question arose as to what position Acheson should take on the issue. Luke Battle was the member of the State Department Secretariat assigned to work directly with the Secretary as his personal assistant. One day Luke called me to tell me his suspicion that Acheson was preparing a personal statement on the Hiss case and that he refused to discuss it with him. Luke asked me to see Acheson about the matter. I went in to see Acheson, but he asked me to leave. I called Chip Bohlen, who at the time was serving as counselor to the secretary, but Acheson refused to see him as well.

Dean was a close friend of Alger's brother Donald, a partner in Covington and Burling, but knew Alger only slightly. Alger had worked for him briefly in 1946 as liaison with the United Nations. I knew Alger better than Dean from the days when I shared a car pool with him. Chip had his own reasons to suspect Alger. He had served as interpreter for Roosevelt at Yalta, where Alger also had been present. After reading a transcript of Alger's testimony before a Senate subcommittee investigating his loyalty,

Chip came to the conclusion that Alger had knowingly lied in the testimony about some of what had taken place at Yalta.

Luke, Chip, and I all had the same concern. Acheson, we feared, out of loyalty to Alger's brother and without adequate knowledge of Alger himself, would feel impelled to place his personal prestige on the line to defend the man. Dean was widely criticized, particularly by some members of Congress, when he refused at a press conference to condemn him on the day Alger was convicted of perjury in January 1950. Some years later, I asked Dean why he had refused to see any of the three of us. He said he had known perfectly well what our arguments were going to be, he had already taken them into account, and he had made the decision not to shy away from what his conscience told him to do.

Another one of Dean's strengths was his self-restraint and professionalism in office. Although he possessed a brilliant and cutting wit, he was careful not to loose it, and he placed the needs of the nation over personal feelings. One example was his handling of John Foster Dulles, about whom we shared a negative view.

I had formed my own impressions of Foster during my Wall Street days when he was senior partner of one of the important Wall Street law firms, Sullivan & Cromwell. Harrison Williams, who had become one of the earliest American billionaires, was one of Foster's most important clients. Williams had created one of the largest public utility companies in the country, with subsidiaries serving Milwaukee, St. Louis, Washington, D.C., and northern California. He decided he could further multiply his wealth by creating an additional layer in his financial pyramid. He proposed to create the Blue Ridge Corporation to which he would transfer control of the North American Company and raise a great deal of additional capital while doing so. We in Dillon, Read & Co. considered this further pyramiding to be financially unsound and refused to handle the sale of the Blue Ridge securities he wished to issue. Dulles not only helped Harrison Williams build this unsound layer but then helped him build another even more unsound layer on top of that, called the Shenandoah Corporation. In 1929, the whole structure collapsed and the Blue Ridge and Shenandoah securities became worthless. I found Dulles's role in all this less than admirable.

In 1949, when Acheson was Secretary of State and preparing for the meeting of Foreign Ministers at the Palais Rose in Paris after the lifting of the Berlin blockade, he decided to strive for bipartisan support for whatever U.S. policy might emerge from that important meeting. Dulles had become the principal foreign-policy spokesman for the Republican Party, so it appeared wise to invite him to become a member of the American delegation. When we arrived in Paris, Acheson set up an organizational meeting of the delegation at the American Embassy. He asked Chip Bohlen to summarize the political issues and the State Department's proposed approach to them. He asked me similarly to deal with the economic issues. When we had concluded, Dulles spoke up and said he wished the minutes of the meeting to record that he disagreed with the approach Chip and I had outlined; he thought them too anti-Soviet.

Later, when it developed that the Soviet position was wholly unacceptable not only to us, but also to Ernest Bevin, the British Foreign Minister, and to Robert Schuman, the French Foreign Minister, Dulles asked that the minutes of the opening delegation meeting be revised to eliminate from the record his initial opposition to the State Department's position. When we all returned to the United States, Dulles invited Scottie Reston, *New York Times* correspondent, to a press interview in which he said that it was he who had stiffened the backs of the U.S. delegation that otherwise would have been inclined to take positions too soft on the Soviets.

But Acheson was too much of a statesman to let his irritation and disdain for Dulles be evident. A little later, it appeared that the time was ripe to work out a peace treaty with Japan. If we succeeded in doing so, we would need Republican support to achieve the two-thirds Senate approval necessary for ratification. For some time, Dean Rusk had been serving as Assistant Secretary of State for Far Eastern Affairs, handling with great skill all the negotiations with the Japanese over the treaty. Nevertheless, Acheson asked Dulles to become his personal assistant in charge of the Japanese treaty negotiations. Rusk fully understood the situation and convinced Dulles that he, Dulles, had conceived all the important moves and gave full credit to Dulles for their success.

But on matters not involving issues of national importance, Acheson could not restrain his instinct for the brilliant and devastating remark that others could not forgive. He and Senator Robert Taft were both members of the governing body of Yale University. An important difference of opinion arose over the question of whether all undergraduate students should be required at some point in their studies to take a course in mathematics. When Senator Taft grew somewhat heated in his opposition to the proposal and argued that he had never taken a course in mathematics and, therefore, saw no reason for others to do so, Acheson quietly said: "The defense rests." Taft never forgave him.

I too was occasionally the target of Dean's sharp remarks, although I was better able to place his acerbity in perspective than were some of his other friends and colleagues. At one time, after I had accepted President Nixon's offer to work on arms control matters in 1972 and was deeply engaged in the task, my friends told me that Acheson had been heard to comment: "Paul spends all his time with the Russians; he has gone soft on Communism." I was somewhat hurt, but knew him well enough to know that he was cross with me because he believed that if I had stuck to the main line of policy toward the Soviets and not decided to concentrate on the arms control aspect of the problem, I could have had a chance at being Secretary of State in the next Democratic administration. That expectation I considered to be flattering, but much too sanguine.

Many years later, I failed in my attempts to raise the funds necessary to endow an Acheson professorship on foreign policy at the Johns Hopkins University's School of Advanced International Studies (SAIS). I found that Dean's instinct for the brilliant and cutting remark had offended all but a few of those I had expected would welcome the opportunity to honor him.

Dulles succeeded Acheson as Secretary of State on January 20, 1953. The precipitous decline in public interest in a prominent public figure the moment he has ceased to wield power is a long-standing facet of the Washington policy community. The trait showed itself during the transition from the Roosevelt/Truman administration to the Eisenhower administration, and Dean seemed to disappear into private life. Sometime in March of that year I noticed that Acheson had not appeared at the Metropolitan Club since he had left office. This was noteworthy since he enjoyed having lunch there with friends when not tied up by official business. I telephoned him at his farm in Sandy Spring, Maryland and invited him to lunch with me. He said he would be delighted and that no one had asked him to lunch since he had been Secretary of State. From then on we would have lunch almost every week, generally with one or two others. That is when our friendship matured.

Dean was frank about the degree to which a certain zest had gone out of his life upon leaving office as Secretary of State. He went back to his law firm, Covington and Burling, was given a big office and a big desk, but could not become deeply interested in the problems of the firm and the rivalries among its partners. Only occasionally would he have the opportunity to argue a significant point before the Supreme Court.

Dean maintained his interest in the Democratic Party but he had little respect for Adlai Stevenson, who he considered to be a competent enough staff man but who lacked the stuff necessary for command. He did not really address himself to the problems of the Party until after 1956 when he became chairman of the Foreign Affairs and Defense Committee of the Democratic Advisory Council, upon which I served as Vice Chairman. A majority of the committee, including Stevenson, Chester Bowles, and Ken Galbraith, favored the more liberal end of the spectrum of possible positions. It was Dean's and my view that the Democrats could not win the next election unless they could capture the political center, not merely the minorities, the South, and the Left. Dean, Senator Mike Mansfield, and I were given the task of producing an initial draft of a foreign-policy plank for the party's platform. Our draft received the approval of all the potential Democratic candidates but was changed into a meaningless list of special-interest planks by Congressman John McCormick, chairman of the Convention's Platform Committee.

In 1959, Acheson and I, as chairman and vice chairman of the Foreign Affairs and Defense Committee, wrote a paper entitled

"The Military Forces We Need and How to Get Them." The paper constituted the foundation for John F. Kennedy's position on defense issues when he succeeded in winning the Democratic nomination.

Even after the Truman administration, Acheson's quick grasp of problems, and his precision and clarity, continued to make him an effective advisor and commentator. But his great days were those when he enjoyed "command." When Kennedy was elected president, he offered Acheson the position of U.S. Ambassador to NATO in permanent session in Brussels. Acheson was not a great admirer of Kennedy; he considered Lyndon Johnson, despite his obvious vanity and personality problems, to have greater capacity for leadership on matters of presidential scope than Kennedy. If he were to agree to serve full time in Europe, he would be separated from Washington, and it was the development of policy in Washington that fascinated him. Acheson turned down Kennedy's offer but agreed to be available for consultation, advice, and help whenever Kennedy wished to call on him.

In the spring of 1961, Kennedy asked Acheson to work on the Berlin problem. Since I, at the time, was chairman of the interdepartmental Berlin Task Force, we worked closely together. Some have suggested that he dominated the task force's work during the next five months, and I believe that to be correct. Later, however, the four-nation Ambassadorial Group, chaired by Foy Kohler and including the British, French, and German Ambassadors in Washington, took over primary control of the subject of maintaining access to Berlin despite Khrushchev's threats to cut it off.

At the same time, Acheson became interested in the situation in South Africa. He was convinced that political isolation and economic blockade was not the best way to improve race relations in South Africa and that approach would only play into the Soviet hand in Africa. He wrote Kennedy on the subject of the transition from colonial rule to independence in Africa. His report was incisive but it was ahead of its time and was widely opposed.

A little later, Acheson became interested in Premier Antonio Salazar, the strong man of Portugal. He gained an understanding of what Salazar's problems were and how and why his approach was probably the best way to encourage a more hopeful transition for the Portuguese colonies in Africa from colonialism to independence than merely to acquiesce in left-wing takeovers of power, colony by former colony. Acheson followed that up with a report to Kennedy on U.S.-Portuguese relations that including a recommendation to retain a U.S. base in the Azores. The report also dealt with the Portuguese position in Angola.

Acheson thought that the U.S. should be sympathetic to continued Portuguese influence in Angola, to the advantage of African and Portuguese alike. The UN resolution in 1961 demanding the rapid withdrawal of Portugal from her African colonies, which the Kennedy administration supported, was pushing much too fast, and would leave the African population unready for self-rule. An internally weak, independent Angola would be vulnerable to long and continuous tribal wars, offering Moscow and its satellites an opportunity to intervene—to nobody's advantage—which did in fact occur with tragic consequences. Furthermore, pressing hard for an end to the Portuguese colonial presence would only alienate an important NATO partner.[1]

---

[1] Brinkley, Douglas, *Dean Acheson: The Cold War Years, 1953–1971* (New Haven and London: Yale University Press, 1992), pp. 307–308.

In October of 1962, President Kennedy asked Acheson to participate in the discussions of the Excomm, the National Security Council's Executive Committee that was dealing with the Cuban missile crisis. From the beginning of the crisis, Dean favored forceful action, including air attacks on the missile sites and the air defenses covering them. Later, it was suggested that our first step should be a blockade of the island. Leonard Meeker, the State Department's lawyer, protested that it would be contrary to international law for us to do so without a prior declaration of war. Acheson countered that international law was created by precedent and that in this instance we should make a new precedent, not just accept what in the past had been deemed proper in quite different and less serious circumstances. If the President was uncomfortable with the word "blockade" Dean asked why should we not use some other word, such as "quarantine."

As part of Kennedy's plan to brief our principal allies before his policy speech on the crisis, the President asked Acheson to fly to Paris to speak with President Charles de Gaulle. To maintain complete secrecy, he was taken to General de Gaulle's residence through the tunnels of Paris. Dean had barely begun his briefing and was about to show the General the satellite photographs of the missile sites when de Gaulle told him that would not be necessary. Acheson, he said, had told him the situation; he could now return to Washington and tell the President that he, General de Gaulle, fully backed the President's decision.

During the Johnson administration, Acheson served almost continuously as a presidential advisor on a number of issues, particularly on our growing problems with France and its withdrawal from active participation in the North Atlantic Treaty Organization, despite the fact that the French wished to maintain the political commitments of the U.S. to come to the support of the European members of the North Atlantic if attacked in the treaty area. On Vietnam, Acheson was the principal Johnson advisor to judge that there was not sufficient U.S. public support to warrant continuing the all-out commitment to a South Vietnamese victory that had, up to that time, characterized U.S. policy.

Even after Dean Acheson's death in 1971, his memory continued to exert influence on U.S. policy. In the spring of 1974, I returned to Washington from the arms-control negotiations with the Soviets in Geneva. Henry Kissinger invited me to have lunch with him at the State Department. The pressure for Nixon's impeachment was gaining strength. Kissinger began the conversation by saying that it was regrettable that Dean Acheson was no longer alive to give the President his wise advice. He went on to say that he thought I had been as close to Acheson as anyone else and probably could guess better than others what Acheson's answer to a given question might have been had he been alive. What advice did I think Acheson would have given President Nixon as to how to handle the growing Watergate crisis. I replied that I thought Acheson would have said he couldn't give useful advice unless he knew all the facts. Henry replied that was unnecessary; all one had to do was read the newspaper. I then said that if that had been Nixon's answer to Acheson's question, I knew what Acheson's advice would have been. He would have told the President that, under those circumstances, he must resign immediately. Henry was outraged. As I remember it, he said that that was impossible; under those circumstances, Henry exclaimed, he would be unable to continue to conduct U.S. policy.

Acheson had extraordinary good fortune on his side. He was tall, distinguished in appearance, fortunate in his ancestry, and a product of the Ivy League educational system when it was at the height of its excellence. He studied and practiced law at a time when that was a principal path to a successful career. He reached the peak of his intellectual powers during World War II when unique opportunities for responsible service were open to talented men of his age. He was called on to play a crucial role in U.S. national security and foreign policy with two other men of equally superior talent and character—President Truman and General George C. Marshall. That triad was supported by Will Clayton, John McCloy, Bob Lovett, Jim Forrestal, George Kennan, and Chip Bohlen, men of exceptional talent and effectiveness.

Dean also possessed special qualities that helped him use his opportunities so effectively. I would put courage at the head of the list. It was his instinct to head into the crucial problems, not to delay, procrastinate, or shove problems on to others—despite the prospect of strong opposition. He did not wilt under pressure; he fought back. He also saw the world before him with open eyes and as a whole, refusing to let himself concentrate on any one issue to the exclusion of the overall picture or strategic view. Another important quality was his unswerving support and helpfulness to his associates at all levels. President Truman, General Marshall, and his other high-level associates could count on his loyalty to them.

In his conduct of the tactics of foreign policy and national security, his brilliance, his open eyes, and his courage served him well. In putting together a broader canvas of policy, he needed and welcomed the help of others. In analyzing the Acheson/Lilienthal report that laid the groundwork for the Baruch plan, it was my impression that Lilienthal contributed the major intellectual content. In the North Atlantic Treaty formulation, I thought Lovett made the basic contributions. In creating the Marshall Plan, I thought Will Clayton laid out the crucial ideas. But in all this, Acheson was always an important part of the process.

Acheson's intellectual hero was Supreme Court Justice Oliver Wendell Holmes. He would often quote Holmes to underline his skepticism about easy generalizations and his preference for practical approaches. Holmes had told Acheson that in a satire entitled *This Simian World* by author Clarence Day, one could find as much insight into human nature and sound wisdom as in many good volumes of philosophy and anthropology. Acheson read the book and accepted an invitation from its publisher to write an introduction to a new edition. The book gives such a good snapshot of Justice Holmes's and Acheson's skepticism of generalizations that a digest of its argument is certainly pertinent to an essay about Acheson and, more generally, to the theory and practice of politics.

Day reflects upon what makes us who we are by speculating about what the world would look like if animals other than simians had triumphed. He considers various animals, sketching for each a picture of strengths and weaknesses and how these would contrast with the simian result. The problem, concludes Day, is not which animal was best equipped to rule, but which would do it. This was a matter of desire and adaptability.[2] Simians seemed to have full measures of both traits.

The desire that drives simians and their descendants is curiosity, the desire to know. Day observes that many animals have "some" curiosity, but that "some" is not enough, and in only a few is it one of the "master passions"—an appetite that makes its

---

[2]   Day, Clarence, *This Simian World* (New York: A. A. Knopf, 1968), p. 23.

subjects forget all else and sacrifice their ease to its gratification. Among the simian descendants, observes Day, an excessive curiosity has taken hold in the form of a thirst for knowledge and facts slaked only by books and newspapers. Simians absorb this knowledge much too quickly and not always thoroughly or in the proper order. Sometimes what they learn is simply put to destructive use in wars, or squandered in quarrels over the proper form of government without their learning how to govern. The natural result is disorder.[3]

The same curiosity also drives the continuing search for "truths" and the eventual destruction, in endless cycles, of those "truths," and their civilizations with them. The trick is to understand that no truth is final, and to learn not to build on dogma.[4]

In his essay, Day puts us in our place and holds up a mirror to show us that we are only simians, with all their associated strengths and weaknesses. Who we are, he observes, shapes what we will become. His advice is that we should first accept who we are and then follow that path. We should not have unrealistic expectations or artificial ideals. The standards of purity we have adopted are too strict—for simians.[5] Very sensibly, Day insists we ought to discover what to do being who we *are*, not who we are not.

After having read *This Simian World* some years ago at Dean's suggestion, I was deeply impressed by it. But then I thought back to my college days when as a senior I was romantically interested in a girl from Philadelphia named Anna Scott. She and her friends had become fascinated by a gypsy palmist. Having

---

[3] ibid., p. 31.
[4] ibid., p. 51.
[5] ibid., p. 43.

examined the complex of lines, mounds, and oddities revealed by each of their hands the gypsy had made intriguing and romantic predictions as to their characters and their future romances. Anna insisted I go to Philadelphia with her to call on the gypsy palmist. I did so. The palmist opened my hand and stared at it for five minutes, saying not a word. When she finally spoke, she said: "I can say nothing about this man; he has a purely practical hand." Thus ended a budding romance.

Perhaps my own skepticism of mystics, prophets, and revealed truth springs from my purely "practical hand" and the nature it reveals. But this skepticism is accompanied by great confidence in the human mind, its ability to reason, to foresee, to test the probable consequences of one set of actions from those to be expected from some other set of actions, to build on the experience and wisdom of past generations and to have some commonsense grasp of the distinction between the better and the worse (not the good from the bad, which is too absolute for us simian beings).

Because of my continuing interest in political theory, I was disappointed in Acheson's skepticism regarding most attempts to generalize, to make more understandable the structure of political situations and the interrelation of the causal factors involved. But this skepticism existed in Dean's character with its opposite, a passionate belief in the exercise and practice of excellence.

Dean, in a letter to Philip Watts, expressed in the following words his views on why a career in public life could be so satisfying:

. . . because there is no better or fuller life for a man of spirit. The old Greek conception of happiness is relevant here: The exercise of vital powers along lines of excellence, in a life offering them scope ... Today more than ever the prize of the general is not a bigger tent, but command. The managers of industry and finance have the bigger tents; but command rests with government. Command, or, if one prefers, supreme leadership, demands and gives scope for the exercise of every vital power a man has in the direction of excellence.[6]

It was the tension between these opposites of skepticism and belief that made Acheson such an interesting, successful, and joyous man.

[6] Personal letter of Dean Acheson to Philip Watts, December 9, 1957, in David S. McLellan and Dean Acheson, ed., *Among Friends: Personal Letters of Dean Acheson* (New York: Dodd, Mead, 1980), pp. 133–134.

10

GEORGE C. MARSHALL
AND THE PRACTICE
OF DEMOCRACY

I first encountered General George C. Marshall in August of 1940. In June of that year, I had arrived in Washington to help Jim Forrestal in his work as special advisor to President Roosevelt. Less than two months later, I was back in New York at Dillon, Read & Co.: the president had nominated Forrestal to take the newly created post of Undersecretary of the Navy and, as Jim explained, I could not join him in the move.

Within a week or so of my return to New York, William Draper, a former partner of mine and Forrestal's at Dillon, Read, telephoned me from Washington. Draper had long served as an officer in the Army reserve forces. He had been called up into active service with the rank of colonel and assigned to work as an aide to General Marshall on matters dealing with Army personnel. Draper asked me if I would come back to Washington to work with an Army team organizing efforts for the Selective Service bill. I agreed.

President Roosevelt had appointed General Marshall Chief of Staff of the Army on September 1, 1939, the same day Germany invaded Poland. Marshall promptly rose to the challenge to rebuild and strengthen the nation's defenses. His first task was to complete the equipping of the existing 227,000 men of the Regular Army and the 235,000 of the National Guard, as well as procure the equipment needed for the 500,000 more men who would be called up in an emergency. However, Marshall had to struggle with a Congress reluctant to appropriate additional money for the military and an isolationist feeling that seemed to grip much of the country and many policymakers. Some feared that increasing the armed forces signalled American involvement in the war.

By the summer of 1940 the situation in Europe appeared bleak. Germany had already overrun Denmark, Norway, Holland, Belgium, and France and now appeared poised to invade Britain. There was a growing danger that the United States might become enmeshed in the war with Germany. It was also clear that our small army was unprepared for war. General Marshall foresaw that, should we go to war, we would need to draft millions of Americans, primarily into the Army. Therefore, at the top of his agenda was the preparation of an appropriate draft act, its enactment into law, and then its smooth and effective execution. While the country had experienced conscription in both the Civil War and World War I, the immediate crisis in those cases was clear and at hand. What Marshall and others wanted was a peacetime draft to prepare for war.

General Marshall assembled a small special staff led by Colonel Draper, Major Lewis Hershey, and a few junior officers to help him with this task. They had their offices at what is now Fort McNair in the Washington area. Because of his special interest in the project, General Marshall spent a significant portion of his time in the late summer working there with them. For this reason I had many opportunities to observe him.

Draper had recommended me to General Marshall for work that today would be called that of a systems analyst; someone who can project how a given set of people, talents, organizational arrangements, and rules and procedures can be made to work so as to produce intended results. To help the team it was essential to understand what General Marshall wanted. In the process, I learned from a master how the American democratic process can work in its best and most effective way.

Marshall was keenly aware of the popular and political resistance within the country to any military buildup. He believed that for the public to accept conscription, the initiative for the legislation should not come from the Army but from civilian leaders. Instead of taking the lead in pushing for a draft, it must design a bill and program meriting public acceptance, and then must vigorously support those key legislators to prepare to make the most effective case for Congressional approval.

General Marshall insisted that the program meet certain criteria. The draft system had to be and appear fair, it had to be understandable, and it had to be administered largely by people at the grass roots, local people the draftees knew and understood. The most difficult specific problem was to assure equity between various localities. Some planners, for example, might have preferred to give disproportionate deferments to mechanics and engineers in industrial centers such as Detroit, Toledo, Cleveland, and Buffalo, keeping skilled people in place for the necessary buildup of equipment and material. Other communities with no such industries, however, could view this as unfair. Since the armed services themselves needed large numbers of mechanics and engineers, it was possible to design a process of selection that would surmount the problem.

Once the civilian-sponsored bill appeared before Congress,

General Marshall took a more active role in pushing the legislation. To help muster support for the legislation, he made frequent trips to Capitol Hill committee hearings and became the Army's best and most eloquent spokesman. As Forrest Pogue observes in his four-volume biography of General Marshall, "Few of his contributions to the Army were greater than those he rendered in 1940 and 1941 in explaining and selling the nation's defense program as something above party politics and the bickering of interservice rivalries."[1]

General Marshall's methods in obtaining support for the Selective Service legislation and the needed buildup of equipment and material for the enlarged Army reflected his deeply felt belief in the methods of American democracy. As I relate in my own memoirs:

> To General Marshall American history lived, the Constitution was a vivid and precious document, and the American people were a group whose proper interests and concerns were to be given priority over all lesser concerns. He not only spoke eloquently on the practical consequences of those ideas; he lived them, radiated them, and infused them into those who worked with him.[2]

Marshall's commitment and approach to working with Congress inspired those of us who had only worked as problem-

[1] Pogue, Forrest C., *George C. Marshall, Ordeal and Hope, 1939–1942* (New York: Viking, 1966), p. 59.

[2] Nitze, Paul H., *From Hiroshima to Glasnost* (New York: Grove Weidenfeld, 1989), p. 12.

solvers on Wall Street, and who had little idea of the political constraints of the democratic system.

The Selective Service Act of 1940, which resulted from this work, was signed into law on September 16 of that year. It passed Congress by a single vote and was swiftly implemented. There were many minor problems in implementing it, but I am unaware of any significant group protesting that the draft was unfair or undemocratic in its conception or execution during World War II. Marshall's role in both designing the bill and in getting it enacted was essential.

The question of General Marshall's role in connection with preparations for the defense of Pearl Harbor, and the ensuing disaster, is more complex. Marshall was one of the first to foresee the possibility of a Japanese sneak attack on Pearl Harbor. He was well aware of the limits of U.S. intelligence capabilities. In June 1940, he warned his staff that an enemy could be four-fifths of the way to Hawaii before "we knew that he had moved."[3]

The accord at about the same time between the Russians and Japanese, settling some differences between these traditional enemies, appeared to Marshall to free Japan for a raid on Hawaii, should the U.S. Pacific fleet return to its permanent bases on the West Coast as planned.[4]

Despite the threat from Japan, Marshall thought the defenses on Oahu were sufficient as long as the forces there had adequate warning. General Charles D. Herron, army commander in Hawaii, and then General Walter C. Short, who succeeded Herron, took all the measures thought necessary to prepare for a surprise attack. In addition, the ships then at Pearl Harbor were left

---

[3]   Pogue, p. 166.

[4]   Pogue, pp. 168–169.

there. By April of 1941 General Marshall considered the island of Oahu to be "the strongest fortress in the world."[5]

But in the late summer and fall of 1941 the emphasis in the Pacific military buildup shifted from Hawaii to the Philippines, Malaysia, and the Dutch East Indies. These would be the front lines in any war with Japan, and they became the focus of Army and Navy attention. Marshall chose General Douglas MacArthur to take over the Far East command. Requirements for General Marshall's own attention, including urgent but competing demands for additional forces and equipment in that and other areas, seriously undermined what could be done for General Short in Hawaii. On Oahu, the Army's and Navy's new emphasis upon the Far East seemed to give General Short and others the impression that they did not yet expect a serious Japanese strike on Pearl Harbor.

Accident, bad luck, and misunderstood messages compounded General Marshall's problems during the ten days preceding the Pearl Harbor attack. On November 27, the War Department informed commanders in the Pacific that the diplomatic situation had deteriorated, with almost no chance that negotiations might continue. The department also warned that, although future action by the Japanese was unpredictable, hostile action was possible. "If hostilities cannot, repeat cannot, be avoided, the United States desires that Japan commit the first overt act. This policy should not, repeat not, be construed as restricting you to a course of action that might jeopardize your defense. Prior to hostile Japanese action you are directed to take such reconnaissance and other measures as you deem necessary." In the directive to Hawaii someone added: "but these measures should be car-

---

[5]   Pogue, p. 173.

ried out so as not (repeat not) to alarm civil population or disclose intent."[6] Another message available to General Short was more explicit: "This message is to be considered a war warning."[7]

In response, Short ordered a "Number One Alert," which was defense against sabotage. The alert order was misinterpreted by the Navy men in Hawaii to mean that the Army had gone on "Full Alert." This and other confusions resulted in a total lack of reaction at Pearl Harbor until the Japanese bombs had already begun to fall.

It is hard to avoid the conclusion that General Marshall and his staff had erred; he had been too easily diverted from his earlier correct concern about the possibility of a surprise attack directed against the fleet anchored at Pearl Harbor, and had permitted routine, delegation, and an excess of confidence to lead him into significant error.

By the summer of 1941 I had switched jobs, moving to the Office of the Coordinator of Inter-American Affairs, where I was an assistant to Nelson Rockefeller. My new position had little direct contact with military matters and I saw General Marshall only from a distance. In the weeks immediately before and after Pearl Harbor I was in South America as part of a team sent to reorganize our government missions there. When I returned to Washington, the task of organizing for all-out mobilization was fully under way.

After the outbreak of war in December, 1941, Marshall would have preferred a field command but agreed to continue as Chief of Staff. Clearly he was the only military officer who had the

6   Pogue, pp. 209–210.
7   Pogue, p. 210.

prestige, wisdom, and cool nerves to carry not only the central military role of Chief of Staff of the Army, but also those of *de facto* Chairman of the U.S. Joint Chiefs and U.S. member of the Combined Chiefs of Staff, which included the top British and Canadian military representatives. Of enormous help to him were his simple straightforward rules of insisting on completed staff work, of heading into the heart of each important problem as it arose and never descending to what he called "fighting the problem," and of political sensitivity to guidance from higher authority. He insisted on delegating authority to, and giving consistent support to, commanders in the field. Above all he merited and received respect from all those who worked with or for him.

Throughout the war, General Marshall wore the twin hats of soldier and military diplomat. He coordinated the military efforts with his counterparts in the British and Allied militaries. That the Allies won the Second World War was in significant measure due to his steady and calm leadership.

After the end of hostilities, Marshall's skills as a diplomat were quickly turned to new challenges. At the time of the Japanese surrender in 1945, one of the principal areas of worry for the Truman administration was the future of China, which appeared on the verge of civil war. There had been intense disagreement in Washington between those ardently supporting Chiang Kai-shek and those convinced that Chiang and his cronies were essentially corrupt, that they had little desire to fight the Japanese. Many were convinced that the Nationalists were determined to save whatever military capabilities they had to battle the Chinese Communists under Mao Tse-tung. The wisest observers of the China scene, including John Paton Davies, had concluded that a coalition government under Chiang was impossible and that we should try a two-China approach—Collaborating with the Communists at

Yenan, while at the same time attempting to reform the Nationalist government.

The Truman administration considered unacceptable the domestic and international political consequences of such action and decided that an attempt should be made to negotiate a political settlement between the two Chinese factions. General Marshall, who had just turned over his duties as Chief of Staff of the Army to General Dwight D. Eisenhower, was the only American who had the prestige and cool head to have even the remotest chance of succeeding in the task. Furthermore, he had past experience in China and even spoke some Chinese, having served there in the 1920s. During the war he had worked hard, and often vainly, to smooth relations between Chiang and General "Vinegar" Joe Stilwell, who was assigned to lead the Chinese military efforts against the Japanese. Secretary of Agriculture Clinton Anderson recommended that President Truman ask General Marshall to postpone his retirement and go to China. In November of 1945, immediately after he had stepped down as Chief of Staff of the Army, Marshall took on the difficult task of trying to mediate between the two sides and avert civil war in China.

Serious negotiations followed within the Truman administration concerning the directive under which General Marshall was to operate. The most difficult question was what Marshall should do if Chiang Kai-shek brought on a breakdown of the negotiations by failing to make reasonable concessions. It was decided that the U.S. would still have to aid the Generalissimo in evacuating Japanese troops from North China. On the other hand, no one was ready to commit American forces adequate to deny Chinese Communist control of much of China. General Marshall was thus sent into the negotiations without the neces-

sary means to succeed in obtaining agreement on any course offering a prospect of lasting success.

When Marshall flew into Nanking to be received by Chiang
and his group, he told them the U.S. government would hesitate
to keep troops, ships, and planes in China without a definite
move toward peace and mutual concessions by both the Nationalist government and the Communists. The Communists, under
guidance from Moscow, were removing everything they could
lay their hands on in Manchuria. Both sides continued attacks
on each other's forces. Marshall sought a ceasefire, withdrawal of
the Communists ten miles from the railroads, and Nationalist
government willingness to consult with the Communists on any
moves into North China, except along the Peiping-Mukden railroad. He also proposed the creation of a committee consisting of
one Communist representative, one Nationalist representative,
and one American to proceed to North China and make recommendations on receiving Japanese surrender and facilitating the
movement of troops. Chou En-lai represented the Communists
in these discussions with his usual skills.

For a short time it appeared that the prospects for an agreement were good. On February 25, 1946, an agreement providing
for the phased unification of the Nationalist and Communist
forces failed to obtain the signature of Chou En-lai at the last
moment, presumably upon the instructions of Mao. The fighting again intensified.

After a few military successes the Nationalist generals concluded they could singlehandedly defeat the Communists and
refused to cooperate in moves toward a ceasefire and negotiations. General Marshall told Chiang under those conditions he
could not continue as mediator. He explained that there must be

no question regarding the integrity of his position or actions, or those of the United States, as represented by him.

Just after the turn of the year in January 1947, President Truman asked Marshall to return to Washington for consultation. Truman had decided to accept the resignation of James F. Byrnes, the Secretary of State, and Marshall knew he would be asked to take his place. His personal desire was to decline and retire, but he believed the situation required that he do what the President wished. While some saw in General Marshall a possible future presidential candidate, Marshall quickly put these speculations to rest. His first act on returning to Washington was to make a statement on the subject. He said that he was assuming that the office of Secretary of State was nonpolitical, adding that he could never be drafted for any political office. This statement served to consolidate his already immense prestige.

Dean Acheson, who briefly served under Marshall as Undersecretary of State for Political Affairs, describes in his memoir *Present at the Creation* the type of organization General Marshall sought in the State Department.[8] Marshall did not want the Department to look to him for instructions; his subordinates were to take the initiative in seizing problems that needed attention and then to do the best they could. He wanted Acheson to be the sole channel between him and the Department, in other words, a direct line of command through the Undersecretary. But Acheson believed he should present Marshall with a series of alternatives while still indicating which alternative he favored and the reasons for that opinion.

---

[8] Acheson, Dean, *Present at the Creation: My Years in the State Department* (New York: Norton, 1969), p. 213

When Marshall assumed office as Secretary of State, Edward Stettinius, James Byrnes's predecessor as Secretary of State, was engaged in an effort to salvage an investment he had made after retiring from office in the Liberia Company. That company had been created on the suggestion of Blackwell Smith, a Davis Polk lawyer, to exploit a rich iron ore concession in Liberia. Before they could get the company under way, another American entrepreneur had secured control over the concession.

To retrieve their investment, Stettinius and Smith decided to seek concessions from the Liberian government to establish a bank there that could be used as an instrument to facilitate illegal money transactions. They also wanted legislation making Liberia a haven for "flags of convenience" ship registration. To get the Liberian government to approve this legislation they needed the support of the State Department. The matter came to the Bureau of Economic Trade Policy in the State Department for decision. As head of that bureau, I decided that the purposes of the project were improper and that the Liberian government should be so advised.

I then received a telephone call from Pat Carter, Secretary Marshall's personal assistant, directing me to report immediately to the Secretary's office. General Marshall had just had a visit from Stettinius. Marshall was furious. "Who authorized you to tell a predecessor of mine as Secretary of State that he was a crook?" he shouted. I in turn became angry. "But what he proposes to do is crooked!" I protested.

Marshall called in my immediate boss, Willard Thorp. He recommended that we ask Arthur H. Dean, the senior partner of Sullivan and Cromwell, another prestigious New York law firm, to look into the matter. Dean found that the purposes of Stettinius' project were in fact improper. Marshall's rage with me was appeased. Like most leaders he needed and respected subordinates who would stand up to him.

The turning point in the United States national security and foreign policy after World War II came in February 1947 when the British informed us that they could no longer provide economic and political support for Greece and Turkey. Both those countries were under intense military and political pressure from guerrillas and subversive elements backed by Stalin and forces responsive to his leadership. That event convinced President Truman that it was necessary not only to provide Greece and Turkey with the support they needed, but more generally that the United States must assume active leadership in constructing a viable free world and assist in its defense while it was under construction. In the next fifteen weeks the State Department under Marshall, Acheson, and Will Clayton as Undersecretary for Economic Affairs, began to lay the foundations of the American military foreign policy that was to guide the United States for the next forty years and eventually led to victory in the Cold War.

In March, Secretary Marshall attended a meeting of foreign ministers in Moscow that convinced him that he had been inadequately prepared for the meeting. He had been sent to Moscow with no worthwhile guidance as to how to deal with Soviet Foreign Minister Molotov, who, backed by Stalin, was totally uncooperative and recalcitrant. Upon his return to Washington he instructed Acheson to create a staff to concentrate on the crucial strategic issues and to design courses of action to deal with them. In response, Acheson created the State Department Policy Planning Staff, choosing George Kennan to head it. Clayton, Acheson, Bohlen, Kennan, and my colleagues in the economic part of the State Department eventually evolved the ideas that were incorporated in the speech General Marshall delivered at Harvard in June of that year outlining what became known as the European Recovery Plan (ERP) or the Marshall Plan.

One can say that various individuals, other than Secretary Marshall, were responsible for conceiving and working out specific aspects of the Marshall plan and its execution. But we were all working under his general guidance and he alone was responsible for much of the execution. To illustrate this point, let me recall a particular episode.

One Thursday during the Congressional hearings on the legislation authorizing and appropriating the funds for the Marshall Plan, General Marshall called Chip Bohlen and me to his secretary's office. He told us that he had been asked to appear the following Monday morning at 11 o'clock at the Senate Appropriations Committee hearing room to testify on the appropriations bill. He asked Chip to prepare the part of his testimony dealing with the political issues and asked me to prepare the part dealing with the economic issues. We were to meld the two parts into a single document and discuss it with him the next morning. We did so and appeared with our joint paper.

General Marshall glanced over the paper, thought about it for a few minutes and then spoke. He said he had decided not to use it. Chip and I both showed surprise and shock. "Don't worry," he reassured us. "It's a good paper. I'll read it carefully over the weekend and will know it thoroughly. But what is it the Senators want to know? If I go there and read this paper they'll know it was prepared for me, probably by you two. But they don't want to hear what you two have to say. They want to know whether I know anything about the Marshall Plan."

He went on to say that he would appear a little late at the hearing. He would sit down and they would ask him to present his statement. He would reply that he had no statement, he was appearing at their request and he would be pleased to answer their questions. No matter what questions they asked, he was confident he could answer them well enough on the basis of his study of our paper.

He carried his act off with complete success. General Marshall radiated stern integrity, but he once again demonstrated his mastery of the art of effective presentation. The Committee at its initial session voted unanimously to approve the bill.

Paving the way for Congressional approval of the Marshall Plan often took creativity. Another Thursday morning, the House Rules Committee decreed that the Foreign Affairs Committee should have its report on the Marshall Plan authorization bill in the hands of each Congressman by the opening of business on the following Monday. Nothing whatever had been put on paper by the Committee toward such a report except for a short paper by Burt Marshall, then a Foreign Affairs Committee staffer, that provided a conceptual framework. Burt, Ernest Gross, who was serving as Counselor to the Secretary of State, and I were directed to have a draft of the report ready for review by the committee members the following morning.

That evening after supper, Ernie and I went to Burt's office. He was sitting in the middle of the floor pasting sheets of typewriter paper into a long strip some twenty feet in length. We asked him what it was for. He said that when he got through with his pasting job, he would put one end of it into the typewriter and produce the first chapter. In the meantime, Ernie would be scribbling out text for the second chapter and I would be working on the third. After Burt had produced an initial draft of the first three chapters we would go over them and argue out the revisions that were necessary. He would cut out from the long strip those lines that had to go, type up the revised section, and paste them back into the long strip. By dawn on Friday we had an initial draft for the Committee to go over. By Saturday afternoon, we could send the completed text to the Government Printing Office. I marveled at the skill, determination, and sheer creativity that Burt had demonstrated. It remains the best single document explaining the Marshall Plan and what was needed to make it work.

The congressional language authorizing and appropriating funds for the first year of the Marshall Plan was consolidated into a bill that covered all foreign assistance programs, including aid to Nationalist China under Chiang Kai-shek. I was a State Department witness on that bill before the House Foreign Affairs Committee. The Republicans had won a majority in the recent election and were in control of the committee. They asked me, in addition to being a witness, to assist the committee's staff.

One afternoon, the Democratic members of the committee had left the room leaving only seven Republicans and the staff, of which I was one. The members began discussing among themselves the position they should take on aid to Nationalist China. The deciding argument led by Walter H. "Doc" Judd, John M. Vorys and John Davis Lodge was that General Marshall's prestige was the principal political force sustaining the hopes of the Democrats in the next election. If he could be discredited, the Republicans could win the election.

The members decided that the best way to discredit General Marshall was to appropriate more aid for Nationalist China than the Executive branch had requested. Even with this additional aid the Chinese Nationalist position was hopeless. But this maneuver could shift the blame for the loss of China to General Marshall and the Democrats; thus the Republicans could avoid carrying the blame themselves, although they had been Chiang's principal American supporters for years. Events developed along the lines the Republicans had foreseen, but General Marshall's prestige was impervious to such an attack.

After the Marshall Plan was safely underway, General Marshall again hoped that he and Mrs. Marshall could retire to their small place in Virginia. But that was not to be. He continued to guide the State Department with a steady hand until Dean Acheson took over as Secretary in January 1949. His short retirement was again interrupted in September 1950 when he answered the President's call to become Secretary of Defense.

General Marshall's service to the United States and the world, both as soldier and as statesman, demonstrates that the role of a single individual can be of vast importance to the evolution of an entire era. He played a central and significant role in the outcome of the Second World War and in discrediting Hitler and Nazism, Mussolini and Fascism, and the Japanese professional military caste. The prestige that those achievements earned for him helped lay the foundations for a politically and economically more satisfactory world than might otherwise have been probable. He helped secure the peace he fought hard to win. Stalinist-Communist expansionism was checked, and the Marshall Plan and the creation of NATO brought about European economic recovery and reduced intra-European friction. Some progress was also made in dealing with the myriad problems in other regions of the world.

Certain qualities of outlook and character, as well as certain principles of action, were prerequisites to General Marshall's ability to function successfully as such a leader. His deep belief in the efficacy of the American political system as set forth in the Constitution and interpreted by the courts remained a steadfast help as he sought to prepare the Army to wage war, and in the peace that followed. He also had an innate instinct to subordinate his own preferences about his personal role to the interests of the nation in dealing with the broad security issues facing the United States.

Marshall believed in taking action, even when based on imperfect knowledge. He believed one could learn only from acting, but that the corollary to this proposition is a willingness to adapt course promptly when new and better information becomes available. He advocated turning over full responsibility on a given problem to a designated individual, and insisted that that individual take those actions that the individual judges to be wise and not to expect detailed guidance. He was equally determined to give full support to this designated individual when he ran into difficulties or opposition. He disapproved of people who shied away from dealing with a problem. He thought they should go to the heart of the matter, insisting all the way on completed staff work.

But in studying General Marshall's career it is also evident that circumstance sometimes made it impossible for him to achieve success, and that on other occasions his judgment erred. He learned to emphasize the responsibility of his staff and his assistants to stand up to him when their judgment differed from his. A commander learns more from those who disagree with him than he does from those who agree. He gave loyalty to his superiors and subordinates and expected it in return, always carefully considering the proposals of his staff. But he insisted that once the grounds for disagreement have been fully considered but rejected, those who had favored a different view should loyally fall in line, or resign.

All of us who from time to time had the opportunity to work with or for General Marshall developed the deepest respect for him. We considered him to be a great American and a great man. Later a number of us who had the good fortune to work with General Marshall created the Marshall Foundation. The foundation has erected a library and a museum in Lexington, Virginia and supports a faculty to help educate promising young Americans of future generations in the ideals General Marshall so brilliantly exemplified and the ideals he so brilliantly espoused.

11

GEORGE SHULTZ
AND LOYALTY

During the Reagan Administration, George Shultz was the principal force in our negotiations with the Soviet Union. He joined the administration as Secretary of State in June 1982, replacing Alexander Haig about eighteen months into President Reagan's first term. In selecting Shultz, Reagan made a wise choice. George was a business executive who brought with him a solid background in economics, labor relations, and finance. He also had a distinguished career as an academic, teaching economics at MIT, the University of Chicago, and Stanford University. He had been president of the Bechtel Corporation, the leading designers and builders of mammoth building projects around the world. In the Nixon administration, George had served first as Secretary of Labor from 1969 to 1970, then as Director of the Office of Management and Budget from 1970 to 1972, and finally as Secretary of the Treasury from 1972 to 1974.

While I, too, had served in the Nixon administration, it was as a member of the SALT team negotiating with the Soviets, so my contact with George Shultz was limited. It was not until President Reagan appointed him Secretary of State that I came to know him better and we became friends. When George arrived, I was serving as head of the U.S. Delegation to the Intermediate Range Nuclear Forces (INF) negotiations in Geneva, which had convened in 1981. My contact with him centered on these arms control matters.

In July of 1982, the INF talks were at an impasse. To get around some of the problems, Yuli Kvitsinsky, the head of the Soviet delegation, and I began more informal talks to work out some common ground. This unorthodox set of negotiations culminated on July 16 in an informal attempt by the two of us to work out, without obligation or prior clearance by either side, a set of concessions that, if accepted by both sides as a package, could settle the issues outstanding between us. We agreed to the terms of this package in the course of a walk down a wooded slope of the Jura Mountains that constitute part of the border between Switzerland and France. This episode later became the basis for a world-famous play entitled *The Walk in the Woods*. Immediately after my discussion with Kvitsinsky I sent a message to the new Secretary of State, asking for an appointment on the day following my return to Washington later in July. Shultz invited me to have lunch with him.

I decided I should report the substance of the "walk in the woods" to President Reagan's National Security Advisor, William Clark, immediately on the morning of my return. Bill and one of his staff, General Richard Boverie, received me at the White House. During the meeting, Clark was called out to see the President before I had completed my report. After I finished briefing Boverie, he told me that Clark wanted me not to talk to anyone else, not even Shultz, about the "walk in the woods" until the President had had a chance to be briefed and consider my report.

When I arrived at lunch, I told Shultz of the restriction that Clark had put upon me. Shultz, understandably, was furious. Within a day, however, he had calmed down and he supported the position I had taken.

A month later, when the negotiations with the Soviets were about to resume in Geneva, I saw Shultz to receive my instructions on how we were to proceed. He surprised me by saying, "Paul, don't look to me for guidance on this subject; you know more about it than I do. I have many other matters on my mind and I want you to proceed as you think best, but keep me fully advised on what you are doing and why. I will then be in a position to help you when you get into trouble and will need my help."

Shultz's instruction to me was typical of his approach to leadership. Like Dean Acheson and General Marshall, he believed in delegating responsibility to his staff and subordinates and expected them to take the initiative without specific instructions from above. Also like Acheson and Marshall, he backed his faith and loyalty in subordinates with the support they needed to get things done. His energy, integrity, and knowledge became a source of strength to those who worked for him.

Our relationship became much closer in December of 1984 as we prepared for a meeting with Gromyko in Geneva the following January and were searching for the right basis for reopening the arms negotiations. George threw himself into this work with vigor. He, Jim Timbie, his personal assistant on nuclear matters, and I spent many hours together with him in his office at the State Department going over technical details of arms control and nuclear weapons. We also shared a deep interest in economics and international financial issues that became frequent topics of conversations among Shultz, Alan Wallis, the Deputy Secretary for Economic Policy, and myself.

Beginning with the spring of 1983, Shultz met with Mikhail Gorbachev or his foreign minister, first Andrei Gromyko and then Eduard Shevardnadze, almost once a month. The agenda regularly included arms control, bilateral issues, and troubling regional issues around the world. After the first meeting, Shultz insisted that human rights be placed high on the agenda.

At first, Gromyko tried to push aside any discussion of human rights as being interference in the internal affairs of a sovereign state. But George had a deep belief in the need to address human rights as a basic tenet of U.S. foreign policy. His skill and pragmatism in approaching the problem helped him avoid the pitfalls of the high-toned but ineffective human-rights policies of the Carter administration. Later, Gorbachev tried to turn the embarrassing issue into an asset for the Soviets by claiming that human rights deficiencies were more blatant in the United States than in the USSR, with its full employment, universal education and comprehensive health care. However, with the help of President Reagan, Shultz won that battle.

During testimony before the Senate Foreign Relations Committee in the spring of 1983, Senator Carl Levin of Michigan gave me a thorough grilling. At one point in the hearing, Senator Levin's administrative assistant entered the room and passed his boss a note. After reading it he turned back to me and said, "Mr. Nitze, I have just been shown a statement issued this morning by President Reagan. In it he asserts that the Soviet Union is an 'evil empire.' Have you any defense for this outrageous statement?" For once, my mind worked rapidly. I answered without hesitation, "Mr. Senator, I would have thought there was a prior question: Is the accusation true or false?" Senator Levin was stymied; to say it was true would be to undermine his criticism of the President, but he would be in much deeper trouble if he attempted to prove that it was false. He changed the subject. Later, I asked some of my Russian friends about their reaction to the President's statement about the state of human rights in their country. They said it had an enormous impact upon thinking Russians; they knew the accusation to be true from what they could not avoid seeing around them. That the President of the United States should publicly so state made them feel ashamed.

George Shultz's commitment to human rights also reflected his strong feelings about matters of personal rights and integrity. For example, he did not permit members of the State Department to undergo lie-detector tests, which he felt violated personal rights, a position with which I disagreed.

I had for years been an advisor to the groups preparing the annual interdepartmental intelligence estimates of Soviet strategic and tactical nuclear capabilities. This work required that we have access to the most sensitive categories of classified information. All of us were required to take a lie-detector test. I had no feeling of being mistrusted. I knew the results were not 100 percent reliable. But I knew of no case in which gross injustice had resulted. I remembered a few cases where I personally had doubts about whether a given individual had leaked a particular classified piece of intelligence. Their reputations were then protected by their having passed a rigorous set of lie-detector tests. But Shultz had a different point of view. He succeeded in exempting the State Department from the procedure.

Shultz was a tough and forthright negotiator with a very pragmatic approach to dealing with the Soviets. In May of 1985, Shultz met with Gromyko in Vienna to discuss the state and direction of the INF talks, which had finally resumed in March of that year after breaking down in November 1983. George and Gromyko began a battle of wits as each fought to set the agenda and tone of the discussions. The press was full of stories anticipating that the principal result of the meeting would be to set a date for a summit meeting between President Reagan and Gorbachev. Shultz had a difficult and bruising meeting with Gromyko. He did not wish the U.S. to be in the position of asking for a summit meeting; the Soviets would then try to exploit the request as evidence of weakness on our part and feel justified in making strong demands as conditions for agreement.

At the conclusion of the final plenary meeting, at which Shultz had carefully avoided saying anything about a summit, Gromyko asked for a private meeting with Shultz. George agreed and the two stepped into a separate room. The rest of us sat around outside with little to do for some six hours. Inside the room George said nothing, waiting for Gromyko to speak. Gromyko too was silent at first, and obviously wanted Shultz to make the first move in proposing a summit. Gromyko finally suggested a date and place for a summit meeting. Shultz said he would report the proposal to the President for his consideration. Soon thereafter Gorbachev "promoted" Gromyko to president of the Presidium, a largely ceremonial position.

George was comfortable with himself, and knew well his strengths and limitations. This knowledge gave him an easy assurance that served him well as a leader and as a negotiator. Gorbachev joined us at one of the pre-summit meetings in Moscow in April 1988. He seemed to be relaxed and wholly self-confident. It soon became evident the KGB had given Gorbachev a full report on a top-secret meeting of the NATO Council in Brussels that had taken place only a day earlier at which Roz Ridgway and I had briefed the Council on the approach the U.S. planned to take in our upcoming meeting in Moscow the following month.

Gorbachev began by denouncing the views on arms control I had presented to the Council as being anti-Soviet and unacceptable to him; he went on to denounce Roz Ridgway's views on bilateral and regional issues. Having warmed to his task, he bitterly criticized a recent speech by President Reagan and then launched into a direct attack on Shultz. Among other things he said, "You seem to think you are always right on matters of foreign policy." Shultz interrupted and said, "Mr. General Secretary, on matters of foreign policy of course I am always right." That interjection so surprised Gorbachev that he couldn't help laughing. This broke the ice and put the discussion on a new and wide-ranging footing; we made surprising progress on a number of topics during the remainder of the session.

George's self-confidence in his ability to work with anyone strengthened his relationships with subordinates. He knew the talents and weaknesses of his team and how to get the best effort from them. At the same time his confidence occasionally led him to retain staff or appointees who I did not feel contributed much to our efforts. Ed Rowney had been appointed a special advisor on arms control mainly to placate the right wing. Shultz rarely consulted him. Rowney was present at many important meetings but never contributed much. Nevertheless, Shultz kept him and listened to him.

Kenneth Adelman was a participant in many of the negotiations and in the preparatory interagency exchanges about the positions we should recommend to the President for his approval. Adelman was head of the Arms Control and Disarmament Agency, and thus was also entitled to be viewed as a principal arms-control advisor to Shultz and the President. Adelman, however, was also part of the right wing fringe in the Republican Party and detested Shultz's moderate and nonpartisan approach to foreign policy and arms-control negotiations. He was persistent in trying to get in Shultz's way, and also in mine. But to my disappointment, Shultz never showed irritation with him. He seemed not to wish to be bothered with Adelman. And when on occasion Adelman did make a constructive contribution, Shultz gave him full credit.

Shultz developed a warm and genuine respect for his opposite Soviet number, Eduard Shevardnadze during the Reykjavik Summit in October 1986. Shevardnadze was as forthright as George, and the two eventually developed a true friendship. However, despite his frequent contacts with the Soviets, George often found negotiations frustrating, although he persisted until he got his way.

During the initial day of negotiating sessions between President Reagan and President Gorbachev and the all-night sessions of the experts at Reykjavik, considerable progress was made on a number of the issues dividing the two sides. Shultz became optimistic that a true breakthrough to mutually acceptable agreements might be possible. But during the following morning session the President and Gorbachev fell into serious disagreement. It was decided that Shevardnadze and Shultz, each with a few experts, would have lunch in an attempt to find common ground.

Shultz tried to engage Shevardnadze in a discussion to sound out a basic understanding on several points, but Shevardnadze was adamant that there was only one issue: would the U.S. agree not to deploy the components of a space-based SDI system for ten years? A complicated formula was found that might make that possible; it provided for the total elimination by both sides within the ten years of ground-based ballistic missiles. This was approved by everyone on the U.S. side including President Reagan. The U.S. delegation agreed upon the total elimination of ground-based ballistic missiles because we considered that the U.S. had a superior long-range bomber force; Soviet nuclear strength was concentrated in its ballistic missiles. Eliminating ground-based ballistic missiles would both eliminate the need for ABM defenses and even out the other facets of the strategic balance.

Unfortunately, when Reagan met with Gorbachev, the President at one point became confused and stated that he agreed that all strategic nuclear weapons should be eliminated, quite a different proposition than the elimination of all ballistic missiles; it would have left our allies vulnerable to the superior Soviet conventional forces in Europe. Shultz immediately corrected the President but the damage was done. Gorbachev was convinced that the President was ill-informed or even weak on the issue and that adamancy on his part would pay off.

Shultz's hopes for a definitive success at Reykjavik had been high. He was deeply disappointed by their apparent failure but soon came to a more objective judgment. He came to realize that the eventual collapse of the Soviet position had had its foundation in our exhausting work at Reykjavik.

Shultz's style in running the State Department made participating in the action with him a thoroughly productive and rewarding experience. He emphasized team play, and unlike much of the rest of the administration, he was able to cut back on bureaucratic infighting. The reason was his strong loyalty to those who worked with him. He stood by his staff, listened carefully to and evaluated what they had to say, and acted quickly with his best judgment. His integrity quickly won him the trust of his team.

On the day George left the State Department at the end of the Reagan administration, those of us who had worked most closely with him decided to organize a surprise award ceremony for him. Michael Armacost, the Undersecretary of State for Political Affairs, arranged for a new commemorative gold medal to be struck, which he called the Thomas Jefferson Medal of Merit, for the date coincided with the two hundredth anniversary of Jefferson's confirmation as Secretary of State.

The occasion was a moving one, for we all had come to admire George's leadership, integrity, courage, and energy. As I observed in the remarks I then gave reflecting upon Shultz's time as secretary, we had witnessed the tremendous achievement he had made moving the U.S. and the USSR from being adversaries towards constructive and expanded dialogue. He had also brought human rights to the forefront of negotiations and improved European-American relations. As we would later discover, his years at the State Department provided much of the groundwork for the end of the Cold War.

EPILOGUE

THE UNITED STATES AND THE FUTURE PRACTICE OF POLITICS

After the fall of the Berlin Wall and the demise of the Soviet Union, the shape of the post–cold war world was quickly evident. A world dominated by one large and relatively stable problem—the superpower confrontation—was replaced by a world with many problems of lesser individual import but greater unpredictability. Conflicts in Kuwait, Yugoslavia, Somalia, and numerous other places around the globe frustrate our hope for a more peaceful world in the wake of the end of superpower rivalries. Similarly, a persistent worldwide recession, trade conflicts, and continuing environmental degradation frustrate our desire for a better quality of life. While we made many advances toward solving some problems—conflicts were settled, weapons destroyed, mechanisms for international cooperation created or strengthened—the list of unresolved problems and new challenges is long and daunting.

New conflicts continue to proliferate around the globe as does the seemingly ever-expanding list of areas where additional conflicts threaten to erupt. For every Serbian and Somali warlord, there appear to be plenty of others lurking in the wings. These troublemakers are likely being encouraged by the international community's evident impotence in the face of naked aggression in Bosnia and reluctant involvement in the face of anarchy in Somalia.

Although these new conflicts are smaller in scale than the global holocaust that previously concerned us, they could nevertheless prove quite dangerous for several reasons. First, the arms proliferation that accelerated in recent years has created a world in which even small forces are prosecuting wars of great intensity and destructiveness. Second, many of the cases of ongoing or potential conflict, particularly in the former Soviet Union, involve parties armed with the most destructive of weapons. Third, many of the areas of dispute are inhabited by ethnic groups for whom a number of external ethnically related groups feel particular affinity.

All of these complications heighten the risk that conflicts will spill over borders, drawing in more combatants in uncontrolled escalation. Thus, even if one turned a blind eye to the horrors perpetrated in these conflicts because vital U.S. national interests did not appear to be immediately at stake, in the longer run the risk to such interests would remain.

In addition to the challenges these conflicts pose, the U.S. is also tested by strains in its relations with many old friends and allies. Such strains are inevitable as nations adjust to the new realities of the post–cold war world. In Europe, without the Warsaw Pact threat serving as the glue holding the Atlantic Alliance together, differences put aside in favor of the greater good of allied unity are no longer suppressed. Furthermore, new differences develop as countries assume new roles.

Increased European economic and political unity, as well as initiatives to further integrate European security efforts, create new areas of friction for U.S.-European relations. Old partners are seen as new competitors. The global perception of a reduced military threat to the free world creates similar strains elsewhere, particularly economic conflicts of interest that the Western powers find it difficult to manage.

From the standpoint of security, the U.S. has been encouraged by the progress it was able to make with Russia, Ukraine, Belarus, and Kazakhstan in expeditiously negotiating agreements to control the more potentially destabilizing portions of the former Soviet nuclear arsenal. At the same time, however, the threat of nuclear proliferation continues to concern U.S. policymakers, for a growing number of countries either have acquired or are on the verge of acquiring nuclear weapons. It appears that, in addition to the five declared nuclear weapons states, four nations—Israel, India, Pakistan, and South Africa—have already built nuclear arsenals or would be able to do so quickly. Four others—Brazil, Argentina, North Korea, and Iran—have ongoing research projects with nuclear weapons as the goal, but lack the materials or the facilities for actual production. Libya and Taiwan have in the past unsuccessfully attempted to develop or purchase nuclear weapons. Although Iraq appeared stymied in its own attempt to build nuclear weapons, its ability to advance its nuclear program well beyond the level detected prior to the Persian Gulf War serves as a warning of the severity of the proliferation problem.

Chemical weapons have spread even further than nuclear weapons, with the number of members of the chemical weapons club believed to be in the high teens and growing. More than a dozen nations probably possess chemical armaments, and about a dozen others are probably seeking them. Proliferation of these weapons is even more difficult to stop than that of nuclear weapons, since chemical weapons are inexpensive and relatively easy to develop and the chemicals needed to make them are among the most commonly used in the world. Despite the ban on chemical weapons, the global community finds it exceedingly hard to eliminate this poor man's weapon of mass destruction.

Exacerbating the problem of the spread of weapons of mass destruction is the proliferation of the highly effective means of delivering those weapons—ballistic missiles. Iraqi use of Scud missiles in the Persian Gulf War, although militarily relatively ineffective, provided a preview of the threat on the horizon. About eighteen countries have ballistic missiles, and the number is likely to grow since several countries are willing to export these systems. Furthermore, many countries are developing an indigenous ballistic missile production capability, which will make it tougher to stop proliferation through export controls. In the future, more modern, accurate, long-range missiles, coupled with more destructive warheads in the hands of more nations, will present a growing threat to countries around the world.

Finally, other conventional arms pervade the globe in numbers far exceeding legitimate defensive security needs. In 1988, worldwide military expenditures topped $1 trillion, and they have hovered around that mark since then.[1]

Unfortunately, the arms trade restraints widely advocated in the aftermath of the Persian Gulf War quickly gave way to business as usual. For many of the old Soviet-bloc countries, sale of military equipment also offers a source of needed hard currency. Nations brimming with military arsenals cannot help but be-

---

[1]   1988 figure from U.S. Arms Control and Disarmament Agency, *World Military Expenditures and Arms Transfers 1988*, ACDA Publication 131, p. 1. The Stockholm International Peace Research Institute indicates that worldwide expenditures declined by two percent in 1989. *SIPRI Yearbook 1990* (New York: Oxford University Press, 1990), p. 143.

come a breeding ground of tension among their neighbors and beyond.

The economic problems of the post–cold war world offer a new set of headaches. An intractable worldwide recession has starkly demonstrated the interdependence of the global economy; the U.S. budget deficit, high German interest rates, and other troublesome economic conditions in many countries have hampered recovery. In turn, the current economic problems have heightened the difficulty of coordinating international economic activity more efficiently for the common good.

The struggle to reach a new GATT agreement in the Uruguay round of negotiations provides a case in point. Nearly every government supports free trade in principle, but in the face of weak economies, many are highly reluctant to agree to provisions that would open domestic markets further to international competition. The most conspicuous example is the reluctance of the French government to offend its demanding farmers by agreeing to cuts in agriculture subsidies that grant them an advantage against their competitors.

In the meantime, former communist countries continue their struggle to shift to free-market economies. In Poland, the Czech Republic, Slovakia, and Hungary, the indigenous cultures had not been completely eliminated by communist leaders subservient to Moscow during the years of Soviet military occupation. In Poland, the strength of the Catholic Church helped Lech Walesa stand up against communist pressures. Poland took the big leap to a market economy in one step. The hardship was great but almost immediately the stores were full and production began to rise. The Czech Republic, Slovakia, and Hungary followed more hesitantly. As we have already seen, in the former Soviet Union, particularly in Russia, the problem is much more serious and solutions are more problematic because of decades of ingrained belief that individual ownership of property is illegal and improper.

The problems of the West make these problems of economic transition in central and eastern Europe, difficult enough in normal times, all the more painful. The basic international economic challenge is to produce greater coordination of global economic activity, including stable exchange rates, consistent interest rates, fairer and freer trading practices, and a more coordinated Western effort with fairer burden sharing to assist economic transitions in Eastern Europe and the former Soviet Union. But the U.S. needs desperately to put its own economic house in order as well.

To help alleviate the U.S. deficit, what is needed is a carbon tax that is equivalent to perhaps fifty cents a gallon on gasoline sales. It would raise needed revenues, reduce our need for petroleum imports, and would reduce the pressure on the environment. If such a tax proves politically impossible, a value-added tax would at least help raise revenues. In any case, more economies will be called for, including caps or even reductions in entitlements.

Besides the new economic problems which capture the attention of the world, there are threats to the world environment such as global warming, ozone depletion, and the appalling rate of reduction in the number of species inhabiting our planet. Deforestation and the buildup of carbon dioxide and other so-called "greenhouse gases" resulting from fossil-fuel consumption threaten to warm the atmosphere, altering patterns of precipitation and local climates in unpredictable ways. Such changes are likely to have drastic effects on agriculture, coastal erosion, water supplies, and the habitats of humans and other creatures. The surprising discovery of the hole in the protective layer of ozone in the stratosphere illustrates the unintended effects human activities can have on the earth.

Other unforeseen effects of supposedly safe activities probably remain to be discovered. Chemicals released into the environment with little apparent effect today might actually become "chemical time bombs," accumulating over time and suddenly creating serious problems as thresholds of safety are surpassed. It has been evident for many years, however, that a range of man-made products and toxic byproducts generated in the production process threaten our ecology. Agricultural pesticides, air pollutants, industrial wastes, and other results of modern economic activity foul the soil, air, and water in many areas of the globe. Even though efforts to reduce the environmental impacts of these activities through regulation and other mechanisms have had some beneficial effects, the damage already done is immense.

The extinction of species through loss of habitat and other conditions created by human activities threatens genetic diversity as well as the biological, economic, and human health benefits that such diversity provides. Other natural resources that were usually considered renewable, such as fisheries and forests, are also endangered. They are being depleted beyond the level of sustainability, and many face total destruction.

The explosive growth in human population is probably the cause of much of the environmental stress plaguing the global ecology. The consequences of this phenomenon, both the large shift of population distribution further toward the developing world and the increased demand for resources, will have profound effects on any attempts to mitigate the environmental damage already done. A billion people will be added to the earth between 1989 and 1999, raising its human burden from five to six billion. By the end of the century, a full 80 percent of the world's people will live in the developing world, and most of the additional billion will live in poverty. This tremendous growth will thus be concentrated in regions where governments and economies are least capable of relieving the strain on environmental resources that it would create.

In sum, the post–cold war world faces a future that will test us strongly politically, militarily, economically, and environmentally. When one considers as well the other problems at hand, such as terrorism, drugs, and hunger, the magnitude of the task before us becomes quite evident.

The experience of the past few years highlights the need for American leadership in overcoming the challenges of the post–Cold War world. It was highly unlikely that Saddam Hussein could have been dislodged from Kuwait in the absence of the role played by the United States in creating and leading the coalition opposing Iraq in the Persian Gulf War. Perhaps nothing short of large-scale military intervention could have prevented the civil war in Yugoslavia, but the attempt by the Bush Administration to cede the lead to the European Community in responding to this crisis demonstrates how ill-prepared the Europeans are for such a role. Our relationship with our global friends and allies has changed and will continue to do so. We are less the protector and dominator, and more the coalition-builder and persuader. However redefined the role might be, the mantle of leadership still tends to fall to the United States even though there are situations in which it would be wise for the United States to forego that role.

The continuing need for American engagement becomes clearer as one considers the resources various countries possess for responding to some of the problems highlighted above. Despite the agreements negotiated between the U.S. and the former Soviet republics, Russia, and perhaps one or two of the other former Soviet states, will retain for years a large and modern force of long-range nuclear weapons. Thus, they will continue to present a potential threat to the United States and to its friends and allies everywhere. To deal with the problem of these nuclear weapons, the United States must strive to maintain forces, both to deter use of the former Soviet weapons and to provide the necessary leverage to continue to negotiate their reduction in a stabilizing manner. No other country is capable of relieving Washington of this burden. And none is likely to be able to do so in the future, nor would it be desirable for any other country to deploy the nuclear arsenal needed to assume that role alone. Therefore, in the future as much as in the past, this remains a task that we may be able to share with others but not be able to avoid totally.

On the European continent, nationalist tensions could erupt into civil warfare and ongoing conflicts could spill over borders. Peace throughout Europe and beyond could be threatened. Some strong nation is needed to encourage and facilitate the peaceful resolution of tensions and, where warfare might erupt, to contain and terminate the conflicts quickly.

In the absence of the United States, Germany has the greatest military, political, and economic clout in Europe. But leadership in maintaining a European peace is not a role for which Germany is well suited. Suspicions of German intentions, whether justified or not, remain too high among the nations of Europe for Germany to be effective in the role of honest broker. France, and especially, Britain, are hampered by economic difficulties. International agencies, such as the Conference on Security and

Cooperation in Europe (CSCE), are hamstrung by their need for consensus. Therefore, it appears that the United States should remain in a position to contribute to the peacekeeping task if the European nations, including Germany, wish it to do so. This does not necessarily mean the continued presence of large numbers of American troops in Europe; Washington should keep only such forces there as are wanted and for only as long as they are wanted. A constructive U.S. role in European affairs could derive from much more than just the number of forces deployed.

Similar examples of problems meriting a U.S. role exist in other regions of the world. In the Far East, the leading role could, perhaps, in time be assumed by Japan. But this would raise considerable concern among other Asian nations, especially those who have fallen under Japanese domination in the past. Further, it is doubtful whether the Japanese would find it feasible to consider the interests of others as comparable to their own. In the Middle East, the unique qualifications of the United States to play a central role have never been more evident than during the events that followed the Iraqi invasion of Kuwait.

For certain problems that transcend regions, such as global economic and environmental concerns, the sheer size of the U.S. economy makes a central U.S. role unavoidable. With more than twenty percent of the world's gross national product, America could serve either as a catalyst or a brake for economic activity worldwide. This, in addition to its leadership in the World Bank and the International Monetary Fund, allows it significant influence over the direction and vision of international efforts for economic development and poverty reduction.

Similarly, the magnitude of U.S. industrial and agricultural activity means that the extent of American efforts to reduce man-made pollution will either make a significant contribution to environmental restoration or would be a considerable barrier to it. For example, a 1991 study of relative national contributions to global warming rated the United States as the worst offender, accounting for 17 percent of the increase in greenhouse-gas emissions during 1988.[2]

Another example is the immense U.S. consumption of raw materials; one estimate found that, between 1940 and 1976, the United States consumed more minerals than did all of humanity up to 1940. Not only has the extraction and use of these materials caused significant environmental damage worldwide, this level of consumption generates high levels of waste. The United States is the world's top producer of garbage.

In spite of, or perhaps because of, these large-scale contributions to environmental degradation, the United States has set the pace in establishing institutions and regulations to halt and reverse damage to the ecology. The U.S. regulatory approach to environmental protection has been the model for many nations that have subsequently surpassed U.S. efforts. Americans also possess great expertise on cleanup techniques. This capability could permit the United States to be an important participant and innovator in the environmental area, especially in terms of training and institutional development. All of this argues for a strong American role in the global arena. It highlights the need to create a generation of Americans who would be capable of assisting our country to participate effectively in such a role.

My purpose in writing this book is to offer some insights and

[2]   Hammond, Allen L., Eric Rodenburg, and William Moomaw, "Calculating National Accountability for Climate Change," *Environment*, Vol. 33, No. 1 (January/February 1991), p. 14, table 1.

guidelines in the form of a theory of politics to help the next generations of American leaders address the problems of the future. I have outlined a simple structure of four interacting elements with which one may interpret political events and apply that interpretation to the world of practice. I have also tried to provide insight into the ethical and moral guidelines of policymaking. While I cannot claim that these insights offer a clear understanding and solution to all the problems with which a policymaker may be faced, they do provide him or her with a starting point and a structure of analysis and possible action.

In the fall of 1992, after I had had an opportunity to present some of my ideas on the theory and practice of politics to the congregation of my grandfather's Zion Lutheran Church in Baltimore, Maryland, a man in the audience arose, summarized his understanding of my main points and ended by quite understandably challenging me to apply them to a current problem, specifically to the situation in Yugoslavia.

In my reply, upon which I later elaborated in testimony before Senator Joseph R. Biden's (D-Del) Subcommittee on European Affairs of the Senate Foreign Relations Committee, I took the viewpoint of an American observer looking at the chaos of Yugoslavia and concerned about its future as well as about the potential long-term global effect of the decisions we might make. I suggested that the first task is to look at the general situation and then to develop a strategic concept and goal, identifying the threat and outlining a general strategy of action to deal with it. The second task is to develop the complex of tactical approaches that appear appropriate to each facet of the task and appear to be practical and cost-effective within the political, military, and economic means.

Looking at Yugoslavia and Bosnia, what is the heart of the problem there and what strategic concept comes to mind to deal with it? The heart of the problem seems to be Milošević and his two gangster associates. He is the worst kind of Marxist-Stalinist tyrant. He is not only ruining what remains of Yugoslavia, including Bosnia, but he is also ruining Serbia itself. Much of the youth of Serbia has been killed; those who remain alive are reported to have become totally brutalized. Economically, Serbia is a disaster area; it is suffering from hyperinflation with little prospect of reversal. Milošević is guilty of mass murder, genocide and organized mass rape of thousands of women.

There is an obvious and simple strategic concept pertinent to Bosnia. It is to get rid of Milošević and his two gangster henchmen, preferably by the Serbs themselves but, if necessary, by whatever means are practicable.

The tactical objectives are many:

1. The most important are political and psychological. They include deepening and widening the coalition of those who are against Milošević while isolating him and narrowing the number of his supporters and thus his political base.
2. They also include augmenting and exacerbating the economic problems of Milošević and his supporters. This can include reinforcing the blockade of the areas controlled by Milošević, denying him financial support, and disrupting his logistic support and his production facilities by selective air attack.
3. We should also participate with our NATO and Russian allies in using other forms of military force to help implement UN resolutions concerning Serbia and Bosnia. It would be unwise to commit significant ground forces in Yugoslavia; therefore, we should do our fair share as participants with our NATO and Russian allies in military ground action—it is unlikely

that many of them will be willing to commit significant forces—but we should not do more than our fair share.

The above program is unlikely to produce quick results because of Milošević's current political support within Serbia. Persistence and perseverance among the coalition of forces opposing him are likely to be the keys to success. Eventual success, if we and our allies keep at it, should be almost certain.

My recommendations for U.S. action would be: our public statements should be low-key and should stress participation with our allies. We should shy away from exaggerated claims of U.S. leadership in this case. My view is that the positions that have recently been taken by the Clinton Administration and by Senator Biden are consistent with the above.

The problems that will remain if and when Milošević has been removed by coalition action cannot be clearly foreseen, but undoubtedly will be great. It seems probable, however, that they will be fewer and less serious without Milošević than with him. It seems wiser for the United States and its partners to act than to delay, despite the fact that it is unclear how they will extricate themselves from indefinite involvement. Not to act would allow the situation to deteriorate still further, and possibly spill over into other feuds.

The complexities of approaching the crisis in Yugoslavia comprise only one of the many problems that will demand American decisiveness and action in the post–cold war practice of politics. To repeat Goethe's maxim, one's duty is to act in response to the immediate problems; it is only by action that one learns what more needs to be done, and it is action that keeps one in touch with reality. The tension between opposites remains unresolved and provides energy for further action.

BIBLIOGRAPHY

Acheson, Dean. *Present at the Creation: My Years in the State Department*. New York: Norton, 1969.

Berlin, Isaiah. *The Crooked Timber of Humanity: Chapters in the History of Ideas*. New York: A. A. Knopf, 1991.

Bland, Larry I., ed. *George C. Marshall: Interviews and Reminiscences*. Lexington, Virginia: George C. Marshall Research Foundation, 1991.

Bloom, Allan D. *The Closing of the American Mind*. New York: Simon and Schuster, 1987.

Brecht, Arnold. *Political Theory: The Foundations of Twentieth-Century Political Thought*. Princeton, New Jersey: Princeton University Press, 1959.

Brinkley, Douglas. *Dean Acheson: The Cold War Years, 1953–1971*. New Haven and London: Yale University Press, 1992.

Day, Clarence. *This Simian World*. New York: A. A. Knopf, 1968.

Doder, Dusko and Louise Branson. *Gorbachev : Heretic in the Kremlin*. New York: Viking, 1990.

Durkheim, Emile. *Sociology and Philosophy*. Glencoe, Illinois: Free Press, 1953.

Durkheim, Emile. *Suicide: A Study in Sociology*. Glencoe, Illinois: Free Press, 1951.

Fox, William T. R. *Theoretical Aspects of International Relations*. Notre Dame, Indiana: University of Notre Dame Press, 1959.

Gutner, Tammi L. *The Story of SAIS*. Washington: School of Advanced International Studies, Johns Hopkins University, 1987.

Hogg, Quintin (Lord Hailsham). *The Door Wherein I Went*. London: Collins, 1975.

Kennan, George F. *Around the Cragged Hill: A Personal and Political Philosophy*. New York: W. W. Norton, 1993.

————. "The Sources of Soviet Conduct." *Foreign Affairs*. July 1947, Volume 25, no. 4, pp.566–582.

Kolakowski, Leszek. *Main Currents of Marxism: Its Rise, Growth, and Dissolution*. Oxford: Clarendon Press, 1978.

————. *The Presence of Myth*. Chicago: University of Chicago Press, 1989.

Marshall, Charles Burton. *The Limits of Foreign Policy*. Baltimore: Johns Hopkins Press, 1968.

McCullough, David. *Truman*. New York: Simon & Schuster, 1992.

McLellan, David S. and David C. Acheson. *Among Friends: Personal Letters of Dean Acheson*. New York: Dodd, Mead, 1980.

————. *Dean Acheson: the State Department Years*. New York: Dodd, Mead, 1976.

Nitze, Paul H. *The Recovery of Ethics*. New York: Council on Religion and International Affairs, 1960.

Nitze, Paul H. *U.S. Foreign Policy, 1945–1955*. New York: Foreign Policy Association, 1956.

Nitze, Paul H. with Ann M. Smith, and Stephen L. Rearden. *From Hiroshima to Glasnost: At the Center of Decision—A Memoir*. New York: Grove Weidenfeld, 1989.

Nitze, Paul H. Kenneth W. Thompson, and Stephen L. Rearden. *Paul H. Nitze on Foreign Policy*. Lanham, Maryland: University Press of America, 1989.

————. *Paul H. Nitze on National Security and Arms Control*. Lanham, Maryland: University Press of America, 1990.

Pareto, Vilfredo. *The Mind and Society*. 4 vols. New York: Harcourt, Brace, 1935.

Parrish, Thomas. *Roosevelt and Marshall: Partners in Politics and War—The Personal Story*. New York: William Morrow, 1989.

Pettee, George S. *The Process of Revolution*. New York: Harper, 1938.

Pickman, Edward M. *The Mind of Latin Christendom*. New York: Oxford University Press, 1937.

Pogue, Forrest C. *George C. Marshall: Organizer of Victory, 1943–1945*. New York: Viking, 1973.

———— *George C. Marshall: Statesman, 1945–1959*. New York: Viking, 1987.

Sobel, Robert. *The Life and Times of Dillon Read*. New York: Truman Dalley Books/Dutton, 1991.

INDEX